WISDOM TALES FROM AROUND THE WORLD

Other August House Titles
by Heather Forest

STORY COLLECTION
Wonder Tales from Around the World

CHILDREN'S PICTURE BOOK
A Big Quiet House: A Yiddish Folktale from Eastern Europe

AUDIOTAPES
The Animals Could Talk: Aesop's Fables Retold in Song
Wonder Tales from Around the World

WISDOM TALES
FROM AROUND THE WORLD

FIFTY GEMS OF STORY AND WISDOM FROM SUCH
DIVERSE TRADITIONS AS SUFI, ZEN, TAOIST, CHRISTIAN,
JEWISH, BUDDHIST, AFRICAN, AND NATIVE AMERICAN

HEATHER FOREST

August House Publishers, Inc.
LITTLE ROCK

Published 1996 by August House, Inc.,
P.O. Box 3223, Little Rock, Arkansas 72203
501-372-5450.

Printed in the United States of America

10 9 8 7 6 5 4 3 2   HB
10 9 8 7 6 5 4 3   PB

LIBRARY OF CONGRESS CATALOGING IN PUBLICATION DATA
Wisdom tales from around the world / retold by Heather Forest.
p.   cm.
Summary: A collection of traditional stories from around the world, reflecting
the cumulative wisdom of Sufi, Zen, Taoist, Buddhist, Jewish, Christian,
African, and Native American cultures.
ISBN 0-87483-478-3 (hc : alk. paper)—ISBN 0-87483-479-1 (pbk. : alk. paper)
1. Tales. [1. Folklore.]   I. Title.
PZ8.1.F76Wi   1996
[398.2]—dc20   96-31141

President and publisher: Ted Parkhurst
Executive editor: Liz Parkhurst
Project editor: Jan Cottingham
Cover art: David Boston
Cover design: Wendell E. Hall

AUGUST HOUSE, INC.   PUBLISHERS   LITTLE ROCK

Naked Truth and Parable

Naked Truth walked down the street one day.
People turned their eyes away.

Parable arrived, draped in decoration.
People greeted Parable with celebration.

Naked Truth sat alone, sad and unattired.
"Why are you so miserable?" Parable inquired.

Naked Truth replied, "I'm not welcome anymore.
No one wants to see me. They chase me from their door."

"It is hard to look at Naked Truth," Parable explained.
"Let me dress you up a bit. Your welcome will be gained."

Parable dressed Naked Truth in story's fine attire,
with metaphor, poignant prose, and plots to inspire.

With laughter and tears and adventure to unveil,
together they went forth to spin a tale.

People opened their doors and served them their best.
Naked Truth dressed in story was a welcome guest.

—H.F.

—a poem based on a tale told in Eastern Europe by the Maggid of Dubno, an eighteenth-century Hasidic rabbi

Contents

INTRODUCTION 9

TALES FROM ANCIENT INDIA

Jataka Tales

The Talkative Turtle 13

The Wise Master 15

A Flock of Birds 17

Tales from The Panchatantra

The Lion Makers 19

The Blue Jackal Who Showed His True Colors 21

The Lion and the Rabbit 23

The Blind Men and the Elephant 25

TALES FROM CHINA

Taoist Parables

Blinded by Greed (Lieh Tzu) 29

The Stolen Ax (Lieh Tzu) 30

The Best Fit (Han Fei) 31

The Powerful Fighting Cock (Chuang Tzu) 32

Whose Dream Is This? (Chuang Tzu) 33

The Useless Tree (Chuang Tzu) 34

A Farmer's Horse Ran Off (Lui An) 35

ZEN STORIES FROM JAPAN

A Monk with Heavy Thoughts 39

The Wild Strawberry 40

Empty-Cup Mind 41

A Dispute in Sign Language 42

Giving the Moon 44

TALES FROM ANCIENT GREECE

Aesop's Fables

Antlers 47

Everyone Agrees to Peace 48

Mice in Council 49

Tales of Mount Olympus

Baucis and Philemon 50

Echo and Narcissus 53

TALES FROM THE MIDDLE EAST

Sufi Stories of Mulla Nasrudin

The Boatman 57

The Smuggler 58

Feeding His Clothes 60

Looking for the Key 62

TALES FROM THE JEWISH TRADITION

Feathers (Eastern Europe—Hasidic) 67

This Too Shall Pass (Ancient Israel—A King Solomon Legend) 70

The Wooden Sword (Afghanistan) 73

TALES FROM THE CHRISTIAN TRADITION

The Legend of St. Genesius 81

Amazing Grace: The Story of John Newton (1725-1807) 83

The Prodigal Son: A Parable from the New Testament 87

TALES FROM AFRICA

Fire, Water, Truth, and Falsehood (Northeast Africa—Ethiopia) 91

The Red and Blue Coat (Central Africa—Congo) 93

Tongue Meat (East-Central Africa—Swahili) 95

Why Wisdom Is Everywhere (West Africa—Ashanti) 97

TALES FROM ASIA AND SOUTHEAST ASIA

The Parts of the House Argue (Philippines) 101

The Tiger's Whisker (Korea) 103

Little Lizard's Sorrow (Vietnam) 106

TALES FROM EUROPE

The Three Wishes (England) 111

The Wooden Bowl (Germany) 114

The Happy Man's Shirt (Italy) 117

The Dancing Lass of Anglesey (Scotland) 120

TALES FROM THE AMERICAS

How War Was Ended (North American Arctic—Central Yup'ik Eskimo) 125

How the Quetzal Got Its Red Breast (Central America—Maya) 127

Old Dog and Coyote (Mexico—Otomi) 129

Paca and Beetle (South America—Brazil) 131

Gluscabi and the Magic Game Bag (North American Eastern Woodlands—Abenaki) 133

PROVERBS FROM AROUND THE WORLD 137

NOTES AND BIBLIOGRAPHY 139

Introduction

This collection of wisdom tales is composed of folktales, parables, and proverbs from around the world. Since ancient times, people from diverse cultures have preserved and passed down homespun knowledge encased in stories. Wisdom tales are metaphorical stories. Their plots can be simply enjoyed for the drama or more deeply considered for the subtleties. Whether comical or poignant, they provide useful insights into life's joys and sorrows and indirectly offer wise counsel for living harmoniously with oneself, the community, and the environment.

Selected from story traditions from around the globe and retold in prose with a touch of poetry, the tales in this anthology contain simple truths, common sense, and the hope-filled premise that we can benefit from the experience of past generations.

A story can be a powerful teaching tool. In folktales told far and wide, characters may gain wisdom by observing a good example or by bumbling through their own folly. A story's plot may inspire listeners to reflect on personal actions, decision making, or behavior. An entertaining story can gently enter the interior world of a listener. Over time, a tale can take root, like a seed rich with information, and blossom into new awareness and understanding. By metaphorically, or indirectly, offering constructive strategies for living, ancient wisdom tales resonate with universal appeal, even though their plots may have originated in a faraway time and place.

—Heather Forest
Huntington, New York

There are no people a thousand years old,
but there are words a thousand years old.

—MONGOLIA

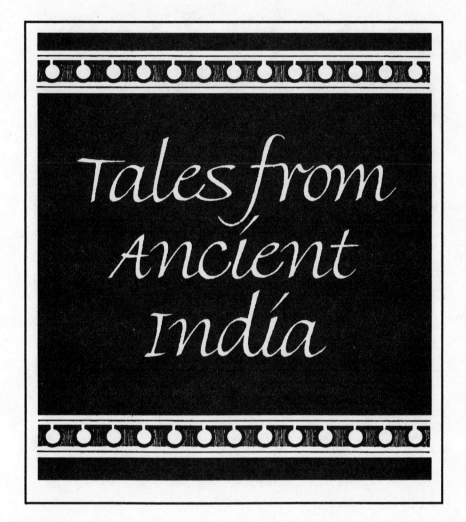

The Talkative Turtle

Long ago in India, there lived a turtle who was always talking. His endless chatter annoyed the creatures who shared the pond, and they avoided him. He spent his days mumbling to himself as he climbed in and out of the water.

One day two visiting geese landed along the shore. The turtle admired their sleek feathers and spent many hours praising their beauty. At last, to avoid the turtle's ceaseless chatter, the geese prepared to fly off to another pond. "Take me with you!" cried the turtle. "I am lonely here, and you are fine company."

"How can we do such a thing?" asked the birds. "You cannot fly."

"Nothing is impossible," said the turtle. "I will think of a plan."

To the amusement of the geese, the turtle said, "It is quite simple. First, let us find a long, strong stick. Each of you can hold one end of it in your beaks. I will then bite hard in the middle. When you fly up together, I will cling to the center of the stick with my strong mouth. That way you can carry me over the trees, and we can land in the pond of your choice."

The geese replied, "What a ridiculous idea! You could fall to your death!"

The turtle protested, "I will not fall. My mouth is strong. I will hold on tightly."

"Your mouth is strong from endless talking," squawked the geese. "You will be safe only if you can keep your mouth shut."

The turtle indignantly replied, "You think that I cannot keep quiet, but I can. I am not a fool. I know when to be silent and when to speak. Admit it. My idea is excellent. Be kind enough to let me try my invention and fly with you."

"Very well," said the geese. "But we cannot guarantee your safety on this

13

journey."

"Then go and get the stick," ordered the turtle. "You'll see how quiet I can be when silence is important."

The geese flew off and returned with a long, strong stick. They each took an end in their beaks. The turtle clamped his mouth onto the middle. As the geese beat their wings and flew into the air, the dangling turtle went up too.

Soaring high above the trees, they were a vision to behold. Some children at play looked up and noticed the strange trio. "Look! Look!" cried one child. "Two geese are carrying a turtle on a stick!"

Another child chimed in, "What clever birds! They thought of a way to carry turtles!"

Another cheered, "Good thinking, geese!"

The turtle heard the children's voices. Their words infuriated him. He fumed, "They should be complimenting *me* for this fine plan, not the geese."

Outraged, the turtle exploded with sound.

"It was my idea!" he sputtered as he tumbled to the ground.

The Wise Master

There once was a teacher who lived with a great number of students in a run-down temple. The students supported themselves by begging for food in the bustling streets of a nearby town. Some of the students grumbled about their humble living conditions. In response, the old master said one day, "We must repair the walls of this temple. Since we occupy ourselves with study and meditation, there is no time to earn the money we will need. I have thought of a simple solution."

All the students eagerly gathered closer to hear the words of their teacher. The master said, "Each of you must go into the town and steal goods that can be sold for money. In this way, we will be able to do the good work of repairing our temple."

The students were startled at this suggestion from their wise master. But since they respected him greatly, they assumed he must have good judgment and did not protest.

The wise master said sternly, "In order not to defile our excellent reputation by committing illegal and immoral acts, please be certain to steal when no one is looking. I do not want anyone to be caught."

When the teacher walked away, the students discussed the plan among themselves. "It is wrong to steal," said one. "Why has our wise master asked us to do this?"

Another retorted, "It will allow us to build our temple, which is a good result."

They all agreed that their teacher was wise and just and must have a sensible reason for making such an unusual request. They set out eagerly for the town, promising each other that they would not disgrace their school by getting caught. "Be careful," they called to one another. "Do not let anyone see you stealing."

All the students except one young boy set forth. The wise master approached him and asked, "Why do you stay behind?"

The boy responded, "I cannot follow your instructions to steal where no one will see me. Wherever I go, *I* am always there watching. My *own* eyes will see me steal."

The wise master tearfully embraced the boy. "I was just testing the integrity of my students," he said. "You are the only one who has passed the test!"

The boy went on to become a great teacher himself.

A Flock of Birds

A great flock of quail lived together in the forest. Food was plentiful and life was peaceful. One day a crafty hunter, who could imitate their song perfectly, came to the forest. When he whistled, a great group of quail gathered in response. When the flock landed on the ground, the hunter approached silently and threw a huge net over them. With a hearty laugh, he slung the net over his shoulder and took the quail to market. Each day he played his trick, and the flock grew smaller and smaller.

After some time, the wisest old quail assembled what was left of the flock and said, "The hunter is skilled and can easily trick you into his net. If you work together, he cannot defeat you. Beat your wings as one, and you will lift the net that binds you."

The flock listened carefully to the old quail's words. The next time the hunter came and threw his net over a group of quail, they were not dismayed. As one, they beat their wings. They rose, taking the net with them. They swooped down onto a tree. As the net caught and snagged in the tree's branches, the birds flew out from under it to freedom.

The hunter looked up in amazement and thought, "When the birds cooperate, I cannot capture them. Each bird is small and yet together they can lift the net!"

The next day, the hunter again flung his net over a large group of quail as they pecked seeds on the ground. Pleased with their mighty accomplishment of the day before, the quail began to beat their wings together. Accidentally, one quail bumped into another and started a ruckus. "Watch out!" squawked the bird. "You are stepping on my tail feathers."

"Someone pushed me!" retorted the other with a hard peck.

"This is no time to fight," scolded another still. "The hunter is almost here. We must all work together and peacefully fly as one."

"You are not the mighty ruler!" sniped the first. "Stop telling us what to do!"

While they squabbled and scolded,
postured and fought,
the hunter arrived
and the birds were caught.
He scooped up his net
and proclaimed, "I'm the winner!
Together they're strong.
Divided they're dinner."

The Lion Makers

In ancient India, four pious Brahmans walked along the road to the royal city. The first Brahman said, "We have studied long and hard. Surely with our great knowledge, we can make our fortune at the palace of the king. As friends since childhood, we should share our money equally."

"I disagree," said another. "We should not share equally since only *three* of us are accomplished scholars. *One* of us has only common sense."

Three Brahmans turned together and smirked at the fourth, who shyly eyed the ground.

He defended himself quietly, saying, "My common sense can be a valuable asset. It is true that you have learned much from books, but I have learned much from life."

One of the first three quickly retorted, "Your common sense will be useless when we have complicated tasks to perform at the palace. It is our great academic knowledge that will earn a fine wage from the king. You should have studied more!"

"Perhaps you are right," sighed the fourth Brahman, who hung his head in shame as they all continued toward the city.

Before long they came upon the dry skeleton of an animal lying beside the road.

"Now," said one Brahman, "let us see how powerful our academic knowledge can be. I know how to assemble the bones of this animal in perfect order."

"I know how to accurately put flesh and skin on this creature," said the second.

"My knowledge is greater than either of yours," boasted the third, "for my studies have taught me how to bring this creature back to life."

The fourth Brahman humbly said, "I do not have extraordinary powers like yours, but I do know that this creature is a lion. My common sense tells me that bringing him to life is dangerous."

"Fool!" cried the three in unison. "You do not know much at all!"

"I know this much," said the fourth nervously. "If you are going to bring this lion to life, I am going to climb a tree."

With that, the fourth Brahman scampered up a trunk and sat watching from high up on a branch. The other Brahmans laughed and jeered.

Confidently, the first Brahman stepped forward and assembled the lion's bones. "There!" he boasted. "I have done an excellent job!"

The second Brahman scoffed, "Wait until you see what I can do!" He crouched over the skeleton and covered the bones expertly with flesh.

The third Brahman said, "Silence! I must concentrate as I accomplish the next truly difficult task." The third Brahman bent over the dead creature and breathed life into its body.

The lion roared loudly and stretched his limbs. Eyeing the three scholars, he hungrily licked his lips and pounced. The fourth Brahman watched with horror from the safety of the tree as the lion proceeded to eat all three.

That is why they say,

> *Highly trained intelligence*
> *is useless without common sense.*
> *Vain scholars in their pride*
> *made a lion and they died.*

The Blue Jackal Who Showed His True Colors

One day a scrawny jackal, driven by hunger, left his pack and crept toward a village in search of food. A fierce pack of dogs began to chase him as he approached the house of a cloth dyer. He dashed into the dyer's house, stumbled over pots and piles of cloth, and tumbled into a huge vat of indigo dye. Heart pounding, the jackal waited until the dogs were gone. Then he crawled out of the vat and crept back to the jungle.

Throngs of animals gaped at his extraordinary color. Dyed by the juice of indigo, his fur was a deep blue-purple. "What is this exotic creature who has fallen out of the sky?" cried all the animals. "He is beautiful and strange!" They cowered in fear and awe.

The blue jackal looked down at himself and admired his own fur. He slyly announced, "Creatures of the jungle, gather around and hear my words! I am your new king!"

Word quickly spread through the jungle as each animal informed the next, "A mysterious creature of royal color has fallen from the sky and is now our rightful ruler!" All the animals of the jungle gathered to pay homage to the king.

The blue jackal was delighted as lions, tigers, leopards, monkeys, rabbits, jackals, gazelles, and others, big and small, bowed before him. "Tell us our duties, O great king!" they pleaded.

The blue jackal began to give out jobs, imitating as best he could the royal bearing of a king. He appointed the lions as his prime ministers and lords. The tigers became keepers of his bed chamber. The monkeys took turns carrying his parasol. The leopards served his food. Each creature except the jackals had a royal task. When creatures of his own kind came forward to bow before him, the blue jackal sent them away with disgust. He wanted nothing to do with them, for they reminded him of his own humble origins. The jackals left grumbling.

Time passed and the blue jackal enjoyed the privileges of being a king. When he was rude, crude, or unreasonable, no one challenged him. After all, he was their leader. All bore his behavior with great tolerance.

One day the jackals began to complain to each other. "He does not give us any honor. We know who he is by his smell. That fancy blue color of his fur does not fool us!"

An old jackal advised, "What belongs to one's nature is difficult to disguise. Even a well-fed cat will still chase mice. Let us howl as a pack and watch how he shows his true colors."

The next morning as the blue jackal berated and bullied the animals who were serving him, the jackal pack began to howl together loudly. Unable to restrain himself, the blue jackal leapt up and joined in with a loud howl too.

The lions, tigers, and leopards suddenly realized that their king was just an ordinary jackal pretending to be what he was not. Outraged at his deception, the animals attacked the blue jackal and drove him away. He tried to return home to the pack of jackals, but they refused to welcome him in their midst, for he had despised them so when he was king.

Alone and miserable, without a family or a community, the crestfallen blue jackal crept into the shadows of his cave to lick his wounds.

The Lion and the Rabbit

L ong ago in India, there lived a vain and ferocious lion. He roamed the jungle and killed for pleasure. To show his power, he killed more animals than he needed to eat. The animals lived in terror of this beast. One day they gathered to decide how they might peacefully persuade the lion to end his evil ways. They agreed that each day, one animal would offer to be the lion's meal. Armed with this brave plan, the animals approached the ferocious lion.

"O Lion, king of the jungle," they cried, "if you will stop your unnecessary killing, we have agreed to send one animal each day to be your supper. Think of it! You will live a life of leisure. You will never need to hunt again. One animal each day shall come willingly to your den."

The lion considered the plan and, to everyone's surprise, roared, "I agree to this plan! The creature who is to be my dinner must come at the proper time. I do not like to wait for my meals!"

The next day the animals sent a wise old rabbit to be the lion's meal. As the rabbit went along the road to the lion's den, he walked very slowly. He dawdled here and there along the way, nibbling at leaves and conversing with friends. By the time the rabbit arrived at the lion's den, it was very late in the day. The sun was setting, and the lion was ravenous.

"Why are you late?" he roared. "You've made me wait!"

"Your Majesty," said the rabbit, "it is true that I am late. However, I am not to blame. A wicked, ferocious lion prevented me from arriving on time. I can picture him now. He had long, sharp claws, like yours, a swishing tail, like yours, frightening teeth and a huge mane, like yours."

23

The lion went into a rage. "Another lion in *my* jungle! Take me to him!"

"I can easily bring you to him," said the rabbit. "Come, and I will show you the lion."

The clever rabbit led the lion to a deep well filled with water. He pointed down into the well and said, "Look, Your Majesty, and you will see the most wicked lion in the jungle."

The lion walked to the well, looked down into it, and saw his own reflection in the water. Thinking it was another lion, he roared a terrible roar: "R-O-A-RRR!"

The sound of his roar filled the well and bounced back to him as an echo. "*R-o-a-rrr!*"

"Who are you?" he roared even louder.

His echo answered, "*Who are you?*"

"I am the king of this jungle!" he roared again.

His echo answered, "*I am the king of this jungle!*"

"How dare you call yourself the king!" he roared with even greater fury.

His echo answered, "*How dare you call yourself the king!*"

This was more than the proud lion could bear. He became so enraged that with claws spread wide and sharp teeth showing, he charged into the deep well with a great splash!

The wise old rabbit went back to the other animals to tell them how the wicked lion had violently attacked his own reflection—and would never be heard from again.

The Blind Men and the Elephant

INDIA

A large, gray elephant stood eating the lush greenery in an ancient, walled garden. It paused for a moment and trumpeted loudly. Just then, three blind men came along.

"What made that sound?" asked the first man.

The second replied knowingly, "That sound was made by an elephant."

"What is an elephant?" asked the third.

"I am not completely certain," said the first man. "We should investigate."

The first blind man went forward with his fingers outstretched until he reached the elephant's rear. His hand moved along the elephant's tail, which graced its posterior slope. "Aha!" he said. "An elephant is thin and long, just like a dangling rope."

The second blind man went forward with his fingers outstretched until he arrived at the elephant's head. His hand moved along the elephant's ear, which rippled with thick, heavy hide. "You are wrong!" he said. "An elephant is not at all like a rope. Just like a rug, it's wide!"

The third blind man went forward with his fingers outstretched until he reached the elephant's knee. His hand moved along the elephant's leg. He measured the girth of its thigh. "You are both wrong," he said. "An elephant is not like a rope or a rug. Just like a pillar, it's high!"

"An elephant is like a rope!" screamed the first.

"An elephant is like a rug!" shouted the second.

"An elephant is like a pillar!" insisted the third.
They began to pound each other and yell.
"A rope! A rug! A pillar!
    A rope! A rug! A pillar!
        A rope! A rug! A pillar!"
Meanwhile,

The elephant stood inside the walled garden,
nibbling the leaves of a tree.
His ivory tusks curved toward the sky,
a miraculous sight to see.

With billowing minds and bellowing mouths
to opinions these blind men held fast.
While the elephant stood, quite undefined,
in the garden of ancient past.

Tales from China

Blinded by Greed

BASED ON A TALE BY LIEH TZU

*T*here once was a thief who wandered into an open-air marketplace. Crowds of people pressed around him as he made his way past the merchants' stalls. Colorful fruits and spices greeted his eyes. Exotic cloths and fine rugs enticed him. Merchants, shouting for his attention, displayed pots, dishes, baskets, and utensils.

He walked on, however, unattracted by the goods until he passed the jeweler's stall. There, spread on the table, was a vast array of golden jewelry studded with rubies, diamonds, and pearls. A wild desire filled him. He wanted the golden jewelry for his own.

"If I had that gold," he thought, "I would be rich! I would build a palace. I would have servants and fine clothes. I would eat only the most carefully prepared dishes."

Overwhelmed with desire, he snatched up handfuls of golden jewelry and ran off into the crowd.

"Thief! Thief!" cried the merchant. "Catch him! He stole my gold!"

Within moments the huge crowd stopped the man. The people surrounded him and held him captive until a guard arrived. The thief was forced to return the gold.

As the guard marched the thief off to jail, he asked, "Why were you foolish enough to steal that gold in front of so many witnesses? Didn't you see the people watching you?"

The thief hung his head. "I did not see anyone. My blindness made me bold. When I reached to steal the jewelry, I saw only the gold."

The Stolen Ax

BASED ON A TALE BY LIEH TZU

A woodcutter went out one morning to cut some firewood. He looked around for his favorite ax and discovered to his alarm that it was missing. He anxiously searched around the wood pile, behind his house, and in his shed but could not find it anywhere.

The woodcutter became more agitated the longer he spent trying to find his tool. Then, out of the corner of his eye, he noticed his neighbor's son standing near the woodshed. The woodcutter stared at the boy and thought, "Look at him lurking about the shed, shifting uneasily from foot to foot, greedy hands stuffed into his pockets. What a guilty look on his face! I cannot prove it, but he *must* have stolen my ax!"

The woodcutter fumed and promised himself he would get even for this crime.

The next day, the woodcutter stumbled on his ax lying beside a pile of firewood. "I remember now!" he exclaimed. "It is just where I left it when I was splitting wood!"

The next time he saw his neighbor's son, the woodcutter looked intently at the boy. He scrutinized him from head to toe. "How odd," he thought. "Somehow, between yesterday and today, that boy has lost his guilty look."

30

The Best Fit

BASED ON A TALE BY HAN FEI

There once was a man who decided to buy a new pair of shoes. He wanted the shoes to fit perfectly, so he carefully traced his toes and heels on a piece of paper. He measured the drawing in every direction and scribbled his calculations around the picture of his foot. He checked and double-checked the numbers.

Finally, satisfied with the accuracy of his diagram, he set off on the long journey to the marketplace. Hours later he arrived at the bazaar. He reached into his pocket and realized, to his great dismay, that he had forgotten to bring the paper with his foot measurements written on it!

Scolding himself all the way, he hurried back home to retrieve the paper. He dashed into his house, found his calculations, and headed back to the market, clutching the paper in his fist.

It was sunset when he arrived again at the market. All the shops were closed. He wailed and moaned as he explained his predicament to a shopkeeper who had already packed up his wares. The shopkeeper laughed heartily and said, "You foolish man! Why did you waste your time going home again to get the measurements on paper? Your feet were with you all the time! You could have just tried on a pair of shoes in the store."

The man blushed and sheepishly said, "I suppose I trusted my measurements more."

The Powerful Fighting Cock

BASED ON A TALE BY CHUANG TZU

The king wanted his prize-winning rooster to be more ferocious. He took the rooster to a trainer with a reputation for turning out champion fighting birds. "Just leave the bird with me," assured the trainer. "Come back in a week."

One week later, the king returned and saw that his rowdy rooster was not crowing quite as loudly or strutting quite as menacingly.

"Obviously," explained the trainer, "he is not ready yet. He is vain and confident. He picks fights with the other birds. Come back next week."

Another week passed. The king returned and noticed that his prize rooster barely raised his neck feathers and wings to incite a fight.

"As you can see," said the trainer, "he is not ready yet. He still flares up and gets an angry look when challenged by another bird. Come back in a month."

A month passed and the king returned to inspect his champion. To his alarm, his fierce rooster looked tame! The king ranted and raved at the trainer, "You've ruined my fine fighting bird! Look at him! He does not want to fight! He'll never win a contest now!"

"That is not true," the trainer replied. "Notice how calm and secure he appears. He stands serene and strong today. The other fighting birds will take one look at him and all run away!"

Whose Dream Is This?

BASED ON A TALE BY CHUANG TZU

C huang Tzu, a Chinese poet and philosopher, once had a wonderful dream. As he lay comfortably in his bed, he dreamed that he was a butterfly dancing from one flower to another, tasting sweet nectar. Drifting with the light summer breezes, he blissfully fluttered with other rainbow-colored butterflies.

Suddenly, he woke up. Finding himself sitting on his own bed, he realized that he had been dreaming.

"The dream seemed so real," he thought. He looked about his crude cottage and sleepily wondered, "Well, am I a man who has been dreaming that he is a butterfly? Or am I a butterfly who is now dreaming that he is a man?"

The Useless Tree

BASED ON A TALE BY CHUANG TZU

XXXXXXXXXXXX

A great grove of trees once stood on the hill where just one gnarled tree now stands. Long ago, the woodcutters had passed it by, saying, "We will never cut a good straight board from that twisted tree." So they let it be and cut another and another.

Then the loggers came after logs to sell and said, "The twisted tree will burn with a foul smell." So they let it be and cut another and another.

Then the carvers came after soft-grained wood and said, "This twisted tree won't do us any good. It is a knotty old tree." So they, too, let it be and cut another and another.

In time, the large, gnarled tree stood alone on the hill. Now during the day, the children come and play in its shade. In the evening, the old men gather about its huge trunk. They sigh and talk about their lives.

"Oh, what is the use of being useless?" one elderly man said.

Another pointed up and replied, "Just look above your head! An entire grove of trees once stood on this hill. Now only one crooked tree still stands, thick with greenery. Had this useless old tree been useful, my friend, it would not have grown ancient with fine spreading limbs!"

A Farmer's Horse Ran Off

BASED ON A TALE BY LUI AN

A farmer's horse ran off, and try as he might, the farmer could not catch him. His neighbor, seeing this, rushed to the farmer's side and said, "How bad for you! Now you've no horse to haul your wood!"

The farmer looked at the dust in the distance and said, "I don't know if it's bad ... or if it's good."

The next day, the horse came back with a mate, a beautiful wild mare it had found in the fields.

When the neighbor saw two horses in the farmer's stall, he said, "How good for you! You must be glad!"

Once again the farmer said, "I don't know if it's good ... or if it's bad."

The next day, the farmer's son decided to tame the new wild mare. The horse threw the boy and stepped on his legs in many places. The farmer rushed into the field, and as he was lifting his broken boy, the neighbor saw what had happened. The neighbor ran to the farmer and said, "Oh, how bad for you! Your sorrow is understood."

The farmer looked up with tears in his eyes and said once again, "I don't know if it's bad ... or if it's good."

In time, the country went to war. All the able-bodied youths were conscripted. The farmer, with his arm around his limping boy, and the neighbor stood alongside the road as row upon row of young men marched off to the battlefield. The neighbor wiped a tear from his eye as he waved goodbye to his

35

own two sons, who walked away with sturdy strides. He turned to the farmer and said, "Say it! How good for you. Your son is home. You must be glad!"

Again the farmer sighed, "I don't know if it's good ... or if it's bad."

This is a story without an end.
Take from it what you will, my friend ...

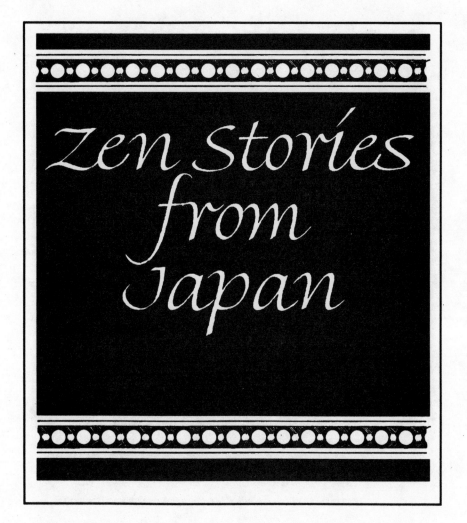

A Monk with Heavy Thoughts

○·○·○·○·○·○·○·○·○·○·○·○

As two Zen monks walked along a muddy, rain-drenched road, they came upon a lovely woman attempting to cross a large mud puddle. The elder monk stopped beside the woman, lifted her in his arms, and carried her across the puddle. He set her gently down on the dry ridge of the road as the younger monk discreetly admired her charms.

After bowing politely to the woman, the two monks continued down the muddy road. The younger monk was sullen and silent as they walked along. They traveled over the hills, down around the valleys, through a town, and under forest trees. At last, after many hours had passed, the younger monk scolded the elder, "You are aware that we monks do not touch women! Why did you carry that girl?"

The elder monk slowly turned and smiled. He said, "My dear young brother, you have such heavy thoughts! *I* left the woman alongside the road hours ago. Why are *you* still carrying her?"

The Wild Strawberry

A man was running, stumbling, and gasping for breath as a ferocious tiger chased him. Dashing for the edge of a cliff, he saw a vine. He desperately reached for the vine and in one last, bold leap swung himself over the cliff's edge.

As he hung dangling down, he looked up and saw the growling tiger on the ledge above him. He felt a moment of relief as the tiger clawed the air but was unable to reach him. Then the man looked down. At the bottom of the cliff far below where he hung was *another* tiger! Tightening his hold on the vine, the man wondered what to do.

To his further dismay, he noticed two mice, one dark as night, one light as day, nibbling at the vine. He knew that it was only a matter of time before he would fall to the jaws of the tiger below. Just then, he noticed a wild strawberry growing on the face of the cliff.

Gripping the vine with one hand, he reached out with the other, plucked the strawberry from the cliff wall, and put it in his mouth. Never before had he realized how sweet a strawberry could taste.

Empty-Cup Mind

A wise old monk once lived in an ancient temple in Japan. One day the monk heard an impatient pounding on the temple door. He opened it and greeted a young student, who said, "I have studied with great and wise masters. I consider myself quite accomplished in Zen philosophy. However, just in case there is anything more I need to know, I have come to see if you can add to my knowledge."

"Very well," said the wise old master. "Come and have tea with me, and we will discuss your studies." The two seated themselves opposite each other, and the old monk prepared tea. When it was ready, the old monk began to pour the tea carefully into the visitor's cup. When the cup was full, the old man continued pouring until the tea spilled over the side of the cup and onto the young man's lap. The startled visitor jumped back and indignantly shouted, "Some wise master you are! You are a fool who does not even know when a cup is full!"

The old man calmly replied, "Just like this cup, your mind is so full of ideas that there is no room for any more. Come to me with an empty-cup mind, and then you will learn something."

A Dispute in Sign Language

Zen master and his one-eyed student lived together in a monastery. One day a wandering monk came to the Zen master and said, "If you will accept me, I wish to study with you."

The old monk replied, "Decide first if you belong here. Go into the garden and speak to my student. Converse with him in any way you wish. After that, come and tell me your decision."

The visiting monk nervously went out into the garden and saw the one-eyed monk meditating. "I will show him how profound I can be," thought the visitor. "I will converse with him in sign language."

Approaching quietly, the visiting monk tapped the one-eyed monk on the shoulder and held up one finger. The one-eyed monk held up two fingers. In response, the visiting monk held up three fingers. The one-eyed monk held up his fist. When the visiting monk saw this, he dashed out of the garden to tell the old monk his decision.

He came upon the old monk at his chores and gasped, "I do not deserve to stay here! I am unworthy of being a fellow student with the enlightened young monk I met in the garden!"

The old monk paused in his work and asked incredulously, "Are you speaking of the young one-eyed monk in the garden?"

"Yes!" exclaimed the visitor. "His knowledge is far superior to mine. I will humbly leave."

"Please tell me what happened in the garden," said the old monk, wide-eyed with amazement.

The visitor explained, "I approached the venerable monk and decided to

42

converse in sign language. I held up one finger to indicate the Buddha. Whereupon he held up two fingers to indicate the Buddha and his teaching, the *Dharma*. I persevered in the discussion, however, and held up three fingers to show the Buddha, the *Dharma,* and the *Sangha,* the community. Then he revealed the limitations of my understanding. He held up his fist to show me that they all are one. I immediately ran here to tell you I must leave." With a sigh, he turned and left the temple.

A moment later the young one-eyed monk stumbled into the temple. He grumbled and shouted, "Where is that scoundrel? How dare he insult me!"

"Calm your temper," said the old monk. "Please tell me what happened in the garden."

The young monk explained, "I was peacefully meditating when that rude visitor interrupted my concentration. When I looked up at him, he held up one finger, indicating that I have only one eye. I held up two fingers, politely congratulating him that he has two eyes. Then he insulted me further! He held up three fingers, pointing out that there were only three eyes among us. I could bear it no longer. I raised my fist to punch him in the nose and he ran away!"

Giving the Moon

O ne clear night, a monk sat in front of his hut on the mountainside, admiring the luminous glow of the full moon. As he gazed upward, a thief crept, step by stone, up the mountain toward him. Arriving at the monk's hut, the thief demanded, "Give me all you own!"

The monk replied, "My hut is empty. I possess only these ragged clothes. Come and sit beside me. I am happy to share the night sky with you."

"Give me all you own!" demanded the thief again.

The monk removed his clothes and handed them to the thief. Bundling them under his arm, the thief crept, step by stone, down the mountain.

The monk sat shivering and naked in the moonlight, watching the thief disappear in the shadows. He sighed and thought, "What a poor man he is! I wish I could give him this beautiful moon!"

Tales from Ancient Greece

Antlers

A handsome stag with majestic antlers admired himself in a lake. As he looked at his reflection, he thought, "My antlers are beautiful! But these spindly legs of mine are so thin I wish I could hide them."

Just then a hunter's arrow whizzed by, and the stag bounded into the woods. His beautiful antlers caught and snagged on the low branches of a tree. Struggling, he finally pulled himself free. If it hadn't been for the exquisite speed of the stag's legs, the hunters surely would have captured him.

After that, when the handsome stag gazed at his spindly legs, his pride would swell. "In times of danger," he thought, "they serve me well."

Everyone Agrees to Peace

A sly fox tried to trick a rooster into coming down from his perch. "Brother Bird," the fox said, "come down for a friendly chat!"

"No," said the rooster. "I'm sure you'd eat me."

"Oh, I wouldn't," said the crafty fox. "Haven't you heard? Everyone has agreed to live in peace."

"Is that so?" said the rooster, who was just as crafty. Stretching his neck, the rooster pretended to look at something far in the distance.

"What are you looking at?" asked the curious fox.

"Oh, just a pack of hungry fox hounds headed right this way."

On hearing this, the fox trembled in his tracks and ran off.

"Come back!" crowed the rooster. "Why are you running away? I thought you said that everyone had agreed to live in peace."

"Well, perhaps those hungry hounds haven't heard about it yet," said the fox as he bounded away.

Mice in Council

A terrifying cat had come to live in the big house. Every time the mice went into the kitchen for a nibble, the cat sent them scampering. "We'll starve!" they shouted and decided to have a council meeting. One by one the mice spoke, but no one could think of a plan.

Finally, a boastful mouse stepped forward and proclaimed his idea to be best. He explained in detail how a small bell attached to the cat's collar would warn them all of his approach. Patting himself on his own back for the excellent idea, the mouse sat down.

The oldest mouse stood up and said, "You are a very clever fellow to think of a plan like that! Now tell us, are you *brave* enough to put the bell on the cat?"

Baucis and Philemon

One morning Zeus and Hermes descended from the cloud-shrouded peak of Mount Olympus and traveled the countryside, disguised as ragged beggars. A long, dusty cloak covered Zeus's radiance as king of the gods. High, wide boots covered Hermes' winged sandals, for he was the swift messenger of the gods. "Let us wander from door to door," Zeus said. "We will discover how mortals treat strangers in need."

Hermes knocked on the door of the first house they came upon. "Good sir," he said humbly, "we are hungry and tired. Please give us your hospitality."

"Here is my hospitality!" shouted the man, who answered the door with a long broom in hand. "I will sweep you away." He swung the broom and, scattering dust, sent the two beggars scampering off his doorstep.

"Well," shrugged Zeus, "we shall try elsewhere."

But the people in the next house were just as unpleasant. "Begone, flea-bitten beggars!" they shouted.

House by house, the two gods traveled the countryside. Everywhere, people turned them away. At last they came to the small hut of an elderly couple, Baucis and Philemon. The two had been married for as long as they could remember and were as coupled as a pair of hands. One would begin a sentence, and the other would finish it. Their hearts beat as one.

As they sat at their table, just about to begin a simple meal of bread and water, they heard the knock at the door. "I shall answer it," Baucis said.

"No, I shall rise and answer," said Philemon. So they rose together, for that is how they did everything. The two opened the door, and before them stood the two gods, dressed as beggars. "Please," Zeus said meekly, "we are tired

50

and hungry. May we come in and share your meal and fireside?"

"Certainly," said Baucis and Philemon together. "We do not have much, but what is ours is yours. We can offer you only bread and water, but it is the best we have."

Baucis shooed a tired old cat off one chair. Philemon shooed a thin chicken perched on the edge of another chair. Together they pulled two extra seats to the table. Two more cracked plates were added to the setting, along with glasses for the water that stood cold in a tall pitcher.

Zeus and Hermes sat at the table, and Baucis cut each a slice of bread. As she poured the water into their glasses, her hand began to tremble. Instead of water, ruby red wine flowed into the glass. Philemon gasped. It was as if the same thought gripped the two like a giant hand. They realized that the beggars who sat at their table were no mere mortals. They fell to their knees before the gods and begged forgiveness.

"We will kill the old chicken! Allow us to make amends. We are unworthy! We have served the immortals food that is too simple!"

Baucis and Philemon leapt to their feet and started to chase the skinny old chicken around the kitchen. Zeus and Hermes threw off their dusty cloaks, and dazzling light filled the room. The two old ones squinted in the glare.

Zeus shouted, "Stop! Let the chicken live. You have clearly demonstrated your kindhearted generosity."

Zeus gathered the two old people in his arms and assured them, "When you have truly given the best you can offer, there is never a need to apologize."

When Baucis and Philemon looked at the table, the bread had turned into the finest meal they ever saw.

"For your kindness," said Zeus, "I would like to reward you with a wish."

Baucis and Philemon wound their arms around each other, and in one breath they said, "We wish to be together always. When we die, let us die at the same moment so that neither of us will suffer the pain of separation."

"So be it," said Zeus. In a moment, he and Hermes disappeared, leaving the old ones to enjoy a fine meal and each other's company.

In the morning, a great temple appeared where their house had been. The two tended the temple until the moment they breathed their last breath together and died. Baucis and Philemon were buried side by side in front of the temple.

Because they gave the best they had to offer, their wish to stay together came true. From their graves grew two trees, a huge oak and a large linden. The trees grew toward each other until at last their branches entwined and gave shade to all who rested beneath them.

Echo and Narcissus

*E*cho was a wood nymph, fond of forests and fields. Her only shortcoming was that she talked endlessly and always insisted on having the last word. One day as Zeus cavorted in the forest with a group of lovely nymphs, his wife, Hera, came along the path. Echo intercepted Hera and diverted her with chatter while Zeus hastily left the woods.

Hera was not deceived, however. Infuriated that Echo had prevented her from confronting Zeus's unfaithfulness, she said, "Echo, you will never speak another word of your own! From this moment forth you will only be able to repeat the last words of others."

In a rage, Hera returned to her home on Mount Olympus and left Echo forlorn in the woods. Echo tried to speak, but to her horror, no sound came from her lips.

Before long, a handsome youth named Narcissus walked through the forest. Echo found him so attractive that her cheeks flushed red with passion. She pursued the sound of his footsteps and longed to express her love. Alas, she could not say the words she wished him to hear, for her tongue was silent.

Narcissus stopped at the edge of a clear pool and bent over to take a drink. There in the water he saw his own image. He thought the beautiful face that gazed back at him was a water sprite. He admired the soft, golden curls that curved around the radiant cheeks and alluring eyes in the water. Soft lips, slightly parted, melted his heart. He said, "I love you."

Echo was ecstatic! He had said something she could repeat and yet truly mean to say. Standing in the bushes behind him and blushing, Echo repeated, "I love you."

When Narcissus heard these words, he thought that the face in the water had spoken. His fingers reached out to touch the image. The image reached out to him. But when he tried to caress his love, the image disappeared in the ripples. Filled with an unquenchable longing, he fell helplessly in love with himself. Unable to move, he gazed at his own reflection until he slowly withered away and died. Hermes came and led his sorrowful spirit across the River Styx to the underworld.

A white flower with a deep purple center grew in the place where Narcissus had gazed at himself in the water. This flower still bears his name today.

Echo, meanwhile, lamented the loss of her love until she, too, faded away. Soon, nothing was left of her but her voice, which is still heard in hollow places, senselessly repeating the words of others.

Tales from the Middle East

The Boatman

A scholar asked a boatman to row him across the river. The journey to the other shore was long and slow. Before they reached midway, the scholar grew bored and began a conversation.

"Boatman," he called out, "let us pass the time by speaking of interesting matters. Have you ever studied phonetics or grammar?"

"No," replied the boatman. "I've no use for those tools."

"What a pity," snickered the scholar. "You've wasted half of your life! It is useful to know the rules."

Suddenly, the boat struck a sharp rock in the middle of the river and began to fill with water. The boatman turned to the scholar and said, "Pardon my humble mind, which appears to you so dim. Wise man, tell me, have you ever learned to swim?"

"No!" scoffed the scholar. "I have immersed myself in thinking."

"In that case," said the boatman, "you've wasted *all* your life. Alas, the boat is sinking!"

SUFI STORIES OF
MULLA NASRUDIN

The Smuggler

A clever smuggler led a donkey burdened with bundles of straw to the border between two lands. The inspector at the border eyed the donkey's bundles with suspicion.

"You must allow me to search your bundles!" the inspector said. "I think that you have hidden a valuable treasure that you wish to sell at the market. If so, you must pay me a border fee!"

"Search as you wish," said the man. "If you find something other than straw, I will pay whatever fee you ask."

The inspector pulled apart the straw bundles until there was straw in the air, straw on the ground, straw, straw, straw all around. Yet not a valuable thing in the straw was found.

"You are a clever smuggler!" said the inspector. "I am certain that you are hiding something. Yet so carefully have you covered it, I have not discovered it. Go!"

The man crossed the border with his donkey. The suspicious inspector looked on with a scowl.

The next day the man came back to the border with a donkey burdened with straw. Once again the inspector pulled apart the bundles. There was straw in the air, straw on the ground, straw, straw, straw all around.

"Not one valuable thing have I found!" the exasperated inspector said. "Go!" The man and the donkey went across the border. "Bah!" cried the inspector once again, scowling.

The next day and the next day, for ten years, the man came to the border with a donkey burdened with straw. Each day the inspector carefully searched his

58

bundles, but he found nothing.

Finally, the inspector retired. Even as an old man, he could not stop thinking about that clever smuggler. One day as he walked through the marketplace, still trying to solve the mystery at the border, he muttered to himself, "I am certain that man was smuggling something. Perhaps I should have looked more carefully in the donkey's mouth. He could have hidden something between the hairs on the donkey's tail!"

As he mumbled to himself, he noticed a familiar face in the crowd. "You!" he exclaimed. "I know you! You were the man who came to the border every day with a donkey burdened with straw. Come and speak with me!"

When the man walked toward him, the old inspector said, "Admit it! You were smuggling something across the border, weren't you?"

The man nodded and grinned.

"Aha!" said the old inspector. "Just as I suspected. You were sneaking something to market! Tell me what it was! What were you smuggling? Tell me, if you can."

"Donkeys," said the man.

Feeding His Clothes

The sultan held a sumptuous feast at the palace. Mulla Nasrudin watched as finely dressed guests arrived at the palace gate. He fingered his tattered rags and compared them with the elegant silks and satins on the people who entered the festivities. His stomach growled with hunger. He thought about the fine food served at the banquet.

Led by his stomach, he walked up to the gate and presented himself to the guards. Since, by custom, hospitality demanded that he not be turned away, the guards allowed him into the feast. The guards, however, ushered him discreetly to a seat at the very end of the banquet table.

Delicious food arrived on great trays carried by well-groomed servants. By the time the trays arrived at the end of the table where Mulla sat, they were empty.

Mulla sadly left his unused plate and wandered out the palace gate. He went to the home of a rich friend and explained what had just happened. Mulla asked, "May I borrow a fine suit of clothes?" The friend gave Mulla rich clothes and an expensive turban to top his elegant attire.

Mulla returned to the palace and presented himself at the gate. When the guards saw him so well dressed, they did not recognize him. Thinking he was a visiting prince, the guards bowed low before him. Respectfully, the guards escorted him inside and seated him at the head of the table.

More trays of food arrived, and servants piled delicacies on Mulla's plate. Before long, everyone was staring at Mulla. He had rubbed curry into his sleeve. He had poured wine on his turban. He had smashed roasted eggplant all over his cloak. Finally, the guest seated next to him was moved to awkwardly inquire, "Pray tell, but why have you rubbed messy food into your fine attire?"

"A thousand pardons," said Mulla, "if my clothes now look the worst. But it was these clothes that brought me all this food. It is only fair that they be fed first."

Looking for the Key

Mulla Nasrudin, the wise sage, crept around in the dust, inspecting the ground. His persistence caused another man to stop and ask, "What are you doing?"

Mulla replied, "I have lost the key to a great treasure and am trying to find it here."

"A great treasure?" exclaimed the man. "Let me help you search for it."

A woman passed on her way to market. Seeing two men crawling around in the dust, she asked, "What are you doing?"

The man replied, "We are searching for the key to a great treasure. It has been lost. I am helping this sage to find it."

"A great treasure?" exclaimed the woman. "Let me help you search for the key too."

A large caravan came along. The head camel driver stopped and, seeing three people crawling around in the dust, inquired, "Why are you crawling on the ground?"

The woman replied, "We are searching for the key to a great treasure. It has been lost, and I am helping this sage and this man to find it."

"A great treasure?" exclaimed the camel driver. Like the others he thought, "Perhaps when it is found we can share it!" He invited everyone in the caravan to help. "Let us all assist you in this important task!"

A large crowd now crawled around in the dust, looking for the key. After a long while of unsuccessful searching, a young boy asked Mulla Nasrudin, "Are you certain that you dropped the key right here?"

Mulla stopped poking in the dust and replied, "No. I lost the key somewhere inside my house."

The crowd stopped searching, stood up and asked, "Then why are we wasting our time looking for it outside?"

"That is an excellent question!" Mulla replied. "Your insight is clear! It is too *dark* to look for the key in my house. There is far more light out here."

Tales from the Jewish Tradition

Feathers

EASTERN EUROPE—HASIDIC

Words, like feathers, fly
in the wind, in the wind.
Reaching far and wide,
in the wind, in the wind.
Careless words, tossed about,
cannot again be swallowed up.
Tongues like swords can cut the heart.
Words fly out.
The rumors start.

Cruel words, like feathers, fly.
Cruel words reach far and wide.
Try and try to gather them again,
but they fly away in the wind.

A woman whose tongue was sharp and unkind was accused of starting a rumor.
She was brought before the village rabbi, protesting,
"What I said was in jest, just humor!
My words were carried forth by others.
I am not to blame."

But the victim cried for justice, saying,
"You've soiled my own good name!"

"I can make amends," said the woman accused.
"I'll just take back my words and assume I'm excused."

The rabbi listened to what she said
and sadly thought as he shook his head,
"This woman does not comprehend her crime.
She shall do it again and again in time."

And so he said to the woman accused,
"Your careless words cannot be excused until ...

You bring my feather pillow to the market square.
Cut it and let the feathers fly through the air.
When this task is done,
bring me back the feathers—
every one."

The woman reluctantly agreed.
She thought, "The wise old rabbi has gone mad indeed!"

But to humor him, she took his pillow to the village square.
She cut it and feathers filled the air.

She tried to catch. She tried to snatch.
She tried to collect each one.
But weary with effort she quickly discovered
the task could not be done.

She returned with very few of the feathers in hand.
"I couldn't get them back. They've scattered over the land!
I suppose," she sighed as she lowered her head,
"like the words I can't take back
from the rumor I spread."

Cruel words, like feathers, fly.
Cruel words reach far and wide.
They leave the mouth a bitter rind.
May all your words, my friend, be kind.

This Too Shall Pass

ANCIENT ISRAEL—A KING SOLOMON LEGEND

King Solomon's captain of the guards was named Benaiah. He served the king with all his heart and took great pride in never failing to do what was requested of him. One day King Solomon heard Benaiah boasting to his soldiers, "I can accomplish any task King Solomon sets before me!" Solomon knew Benaiah to be a quiet man of action who rarely spoke. His boasting disturbed the king, who decided that Benaiah must be humbled.

King Solomon thought, "I will give Benaiah an impossible task. Then he will no longer brag that he can accomplish anything I ask." King Solomon called Benaiah to his side and said, "My heart longs to own a certain magical ring. I wish you to obtain it for me."

Benaiah bowed low and, smiling broadly, said, "Anything you wish is my command! Describe the ring so that I might set forth immediately to find it for you."

King Solomon's eyes twinkled mischievously. The ring he wanted did not exist! He commanded, "Within six months' time, bring me a ring that can make a happy person sad and a sad person happy."

Benaiah had never heard of such a wonder, but dedicating himself to the task, he said, "I will search the world if I must and bring you the ring you request."

Benaiah set off immediately for the marketplace. He visited every goldsmith in Jerusalem, but none had ever heard of the magic ring Benaiah described. None of the silversmiths had seen or heard of the ring either.

Benaiah thought, "Perhaps this ring is from a distant land." He set forth to meet caravans traveling from afar. He approached each trader in precious gems and asked, "Have you ever seen a magical ring that can make a happy person sad and a sad person happy?" None of the camel drivers or traders had ever heard of such a ring.

Benaiah went to the ports where sea captains from distant lands anchored their ships. Benaiah asked each captain if he had ever seen or heard of such a magical ring. Each shook his head and scratched his beard, but none could help in the quest.

Months passed. Benaiah met every caravan that passed and visited every ship that sailed into port. He sought out jewelers far and wide. It seemed as though for the first time Benaiah would fail to do what the king had asked of him. He was downhearted and miserable.

The day before the ring was due, Benaiah went to the bazaar, distraught and worried. He searched the jewelry stalls once again. As he passed a ragged boy with some crude rings and bracelets set out on a rug alongside the road, he paused and said to himself, "I must not leave any stone unturned." He asked the boy, "Do you have a magical ring that can make a sad person happy and a happy person sad?"

The boy shook his head and replied, "I have no such ring."

Benaiah's eyes welled with tears. Now he was certain that he had failed. The boy's grandfather overheard the conversation. He stepped out of the shadows and said, "Perhaps I have just the ring you want."

The old man took a simple gold band and engraved some words on it. He then handed it to Benaiah. The moment Benaiah looked at the ring, his sad face spread with a smile. Instantly, a sigh of relief washed away the frustration and sorrow he had felt during his long search. "Yes, indeed, this is the ring!" he joyfully exclaimed.

The next day at the palace, Benaiah entered King Solomon's court. A feast was in progress, and King Solomon was in a jolly mood, laughing with all his guests. King Solomon saw Benaiah enter and said to himself, "I will not let him suffer long in his humiliation. After he admits that he was unable to accomplish the task I set before him, I will tell him that I gave him an impossible task to do! I shall explain that I did this to humble him."

Benaiah bowed and presented the ring to King Solomon, who jovially took it in hand. The moment King Solomon's eyes gazed upon the ring, the cheerful smile vanished from his face. He looked about the grandeur of his court and realized that someday his life would all be dust.

The simple gold ring he held in his hand was inscribed with the Hebrew letters gimmel, zayin and yud and stood for the saying *Gam Zeh Ya'avor,* "This too shall pass." He knew that the same ring could bring comfort and relief to someone who struggled with grief or misfortune. It was indeed the magical ring he had requested of his loyal soldier.

King Solomon took Benaiah in his arms and begged forgiveness for testing him. He gave Benaiah his ruby ring and placed the simple gold band with the powerful thought "This too shall pass" on his own finger. King Solomon wore the magic ring from then on, for it offered him wisdom and balance all the days of his life.

The Wooden Sword

Once there was a king whose worrisome thoughts swirled around his head like a storm. He feared that his armies would lose battles. He fretted that his treasury would one day be empty. He suspected that his ministers were disloyal. He had no peace.

One day as the king stood at his window, gazing at the crowds in the marketplace beyond the palace walls, he wondered, "How do common people find happiness? Do they worry as much as I do?" He sighed and said to himself, "I wish I were a bird who could fly off and listen to their daily conversations."

Suddenly, the king's eyes brightened with an idea. He called his servants to bring him the crudest cloth they could find. He ordered royal seamstresses to assemble a suit of rags and a hooded cloak. When servants delivered these clothes to the royal chamber, the king sent everyone away and eyed the rough attire. Standing before his mirror, he carefully removed his crown, smudged his face with ashes, and dressed himself in the ragged clothes. He appeared every bit a beggar. Pleased with this disguise, he crept from the palace. Even the guards did not recognize him.

The disguised king walked freely through the crowds in the bazaar all day, observing the ways of common people. It was nightfall when he passed a rundown cottage at the edge of the city. Peeking through the window, the king saw a man sitting at a crude wooden table, eating a loaf of bread. The man's smile lit up the dingy room. The king eyed the meal and the humble surroundings. He wondered, "Why is this poor man so happy?" Unable to quell his curiosity, the king knocked on the door.

"I am a poor beggar," the king said in his humblest voice. "Can you spare some food?"

"Certainly!" said the poor man. "A guest is always a welcome blessing in this house. I do not have much, but what I have is yours."

The poor man's generosity dumbfounded the king. After the two seated themselves, the poor man piously blessed and cut the bread. The king accepted a share of the loaf and watched the man gaily chew the bread as if it were the finest meal.

"Why are you so happy?" the king asked.

The poor man replied, "It was a good day! I am a cobbler who repairs old shoes. Today I fixed enough shoes to earn a loaf of bread."

"But what if tomorrow you do not earn your bread?" the king inquired.

The poor man looked deep into the king's eyes. He saw how the strain of worry had furrowed his brow. The poor man smiled and simply replied, "Day by day, I have faith. All will be well."

The king mused over these words and thought to himself, "This man's faith brings him happiness. He is naive. I wonder how happy he would remain in times of difficulty."

The king left the cottage planning to test the man's faith.

The next morning when the man went out to ply his trade as a cobbler, he discovered that the king had issued a new law. A large sign in the marketplace read, "It is henceforth illegal for anyone to repair shoes. When shoes wear out, people must buy new ones."

The poor man sighed and assured himself, "All will be well." He glanced about the market and noticed an old woman struggling with a bucket of water at the well. He rushed to assist her, and for his trouble, she handed him a coin. As the poor man fingered the coin in his hand, his faith in the future shone brightly. He carried water for people all day and by sunset had enough money to buy himself dinner.

Curious to see if his new friend could be happy without a meal, the king, again disguised as a beggar, returned to the poor man's house. To his surprise, through the window he saw the man eating bread and drinking a glass of wine.

He knocked on the door, and the poor man brought him immediately to the table. The king asked, "How is it that tonight you drink wine and eat bread? I have seen the new law posted in the market, so surely you did not fix shoes today!"

"No, indeed, I did not," explained the poor man. "Today I earned more than before by carrying water for people. The loss of my first profession has made room for my new one!"

"What if no one wants you to carry water tomorrow?" asked the king.

The poor man looked into the king's eyes and simply replied, "Day by day, I have faith. All will be well."

The king left the cottage, bewildered by the poor man's faith. "He has not tasted hard times," thought the king.

The next day when the poor man went to the well, he saw that the king had made yet another new law. The king's messengers posted a sign on the well: "It is now illegal for anyone to carry water for others."

The poor man considered this predicament for a moment and looked about the marketplace. He noticed men carrying wood from the forest on their backs. He approached a woodcutter and asked if he needed an assistant.

"Certainly!" was the reply, and the poor man spent the day cutting and carrying wood to market. By nightfall, he had earned enough to buy bread, wine, and cheese for his dinner.

When the king, again dressed as a beggar, arrived at the cottage, the poor man invited him to come inside. To the king's surprise, the poor man shared an even finer meal.

"How did you earn your keep today?" inquired the king.

"I am a woodcutter now," said the poor man, smiling broadly. "As I told you, I have faith. As you can see, things are getting better all the time!"

The king grumbled as he left the cottage. "I must be far more clever in testing this man. Surely when he cannot buy food for his belly, his faith will waver."

The next day when the poor man went to join the other woodcutters, he found them surrounded by palace soldiers. The captain loudly announced, "The king has commanded that all woodcutters must report to the palace gate to become guards."

The captain shuffled the poor man off with the rest. The poor man, now dressed stiffly in a colorful uniform with a sharp sword in a sheath at his side, stood guard all day at the palace gate. As the sun set, he went to the captain of the soldiers to request some pay so that he could buy his evening meal.

"Palace guards are paid once a month," the captain curtly replied.

With a sigh, the poor man set out for home. As he passed the pawnshop, an idea came to him. He sold the metal blade of the sword for enough money to buy food for a month. "With what I earn by the end of the month as a guard," he thought, "I can easily buy back the sword and return it to its rightful place."

The poor man rushed home and set the table with a fine meal. Before he ate, however, he busied himself carving a wooden blade to fill the now empty sheath he would wear at his side the next day.

The king, once again disguised in rags, returned to the cottage and saw the food on the table. "How did you buy this food?" he asked in amazement, knowing that the man could not possibly have earned any money that day. The poor man explained, "I sold the metal blade of the sword for enough money to buy food for a month."

Never suspecting that the ragged beggar who stood before him was in fact the king, the poor man showed the wooden blade he was carving. "This will replace the blade I sold until I earn enough money to buy it back again."

"That is not so clever of you," said the king. "What if you must draw your sword tomorrow?"

Once again the poor man just replied, "Day by day, I have faith. All will be well."

"I have him now!" the king chuckled under his breath as he left the cottage. "His faith will not be so strong in the dungeon!"

The next day the poor man stood in uniform once again, guarding the palace gate. The captain of the king's soldiers, followed by a noisy crowd, dragged a man accused of being a thief. The captain led the thief up to the poor man at the palace gate and gruffly said, "This thief has stolen a melon. The king has ordered you to cut off his head immediately."

The thief begged for mercy. He fell to his knees weeping. "Please do not kill me! I had no food and my children were hungry."

The poor man, guarding the gate, stood tall in his uniform and calmly considered the awkward situation. He thought, "If I pull out my sword to kill this man, I, too, will be beheaded. Everyone will see that the royal blade is missing!" He pondered a bit more and then solemnly reminded himself, "All will be well."

As the large crowd watched, he lifted his arms to the heavens and cried out, "Blessed be the Most High! If this man is truly guilty, give me the strength to serve the king's command. But if this man is innocent," he said, gripping the handle of the sword at his side, "let the blade of my sword be turned to wood!"

Dramatically, he drew his wooden sword and thrust it high above his head. A gasp went through the crowd. "It's a miracle!" people exclaimed. Immediately, the man accused of theft was set free.

At that moment, out of the crowd stepped the king. He approached the poor man in the guard uniform and said, "Do you recognize me?"

The man replied, "You are the king."

"No," replied the king, "I am the beggar whom you fed each night."

The poor man's face spread with a smile, for he recognized the king's furrowed brow.

The king smiled in return and said, "Tonight and every night, my friend, you will dine with me! Your light of faith can help me chase away my dark fears of the future."

And so it came to pass that the man, who owned little but was rich in faith, became the wise and trusted adviser to the king.

Tales from the Christian Tradition

The Legend of St. Genesius

*L*ong ago in ancient Rome, Emperor Diocletian lounged on an ornately carved chair. Servants brought trays of food to tempt him, dancers twirled to delight him, and musicians played lively tunes to soothe his mood. The emperor yawned in boredom until the actors arrived. Then the emperor sat upright and cried out with delight, "Is Genesius here?"

"Indeed I am!" said a spry young man bounding forward. Genesius was a talented mime and a favorite performer of the emperor's. "Today," announced Genesius, "we will perform the comical play about the Christians."

"Begin!" the emperor said, giggling in anticipation, for this was his favorite play. Since Genesius was especially good at doing impersonations, he easily parodied the characters of his day. The early Christians, whose rituals were unfamiliar to the emperor, were a prime target for Genesius's satire.

The emperor howled with delight as Genesius performed a mockery of the Christian rite of baptism. Another actor ceremoniously dunked Genesius in a huge tub of water, seeming to almost drown him. Genesius came sputtering and splashing wide-eyed out of the water.

The emperor shouted, "Do it again!"

Genesius suddenly stood silent and still. In the midst of the zany mockery, Genesius had in fact been converted to Christianity by the sacredness of the rite he ridiculed.

"I cannot do the play again," Genesius said.

"But it is the funniest one! I command you to do it again!" the emperor insisted.

"No, I will not perform the play," said Genesius, defying the emperor. "It would not be true to myself to mock what I now know is sacred."

The emperor's face turned crimson with fury. "How dare you disobey me! Guards!" he bellowed. "Take this insolent man away and break his legs!"

The guards dragged Genesius away.

In the Christian tradition, Genesius, the mime, became St. Genesius, the patron saint of performing artists. In modern times people sometimes offer encouragement to an actor who is about to go on stage by saying, "Break a leg!" The expression refers to the story of St. Genesius and means "only perform that which is true to yourself."

Amazing Grace

THE STORY OF JOHN NEWTON (1725-1807)

Huge waves washed over the deck of a slave ship caught in a violent storm off the coast of Newfoundland. As the boat listed from side to side, the sea tore the upper masts and flung them into the swelling ocean. "Keep pumping!" shouted the captain as the crew furiously tried to empty the boat's hold and keep the ship from sinking.

Empty shackles clanged loudly against each other on the lower decks as the boat reeled under the power of the wind. No African captives lay chained there now. The captain had already traded the six hundred men, women, and children for goods when he had landed the boat in Jamaica. The ship, now loaded with barrels of sugar, rum, cotton, and coffee, was returning to its home port in England.

One of the drenched crew, a callous rogue named John Newton, had been a sailor since the age of eleven, when he left home to sail with his merchant father. Never before had he been this close to drowning, and he cursed the deadly storm. As he struggled frantically with the others to bail out the water, which quickly filled the vessel again, he dimly recalled his early youth. His mother's voice, reading the Bible to him every day, drifted through his mind. Her comforting words washed over him like the waves. He remembered childhood prayers and, to his own stark amazement, began to pray.

When the shattered ship at last sailed into port, off course in Ireland, John Newton stepped exhausted onto dry land. Barely surviving that storm began a slow but dramatic change in John Newton. For the first time he thought

about his experiences and began to question the meaning of his life. He recalled
how his wild and rowdy career as a young sailor had taken him from ship to ship
until one night, while he was out drinking, British Royal Navy officers had
kidnapped him and drafted him into military war service against the French. He
remembered trying to escape the warship so often that he ended up in chains.
Just to be free of him, his navy captain had traded him as a sailor to a slave ship
captain.

As John Newton stared at the crippled vessel that had carried him into
the Irish harbor, he recalled the first time he had been on board a slave ship
whose lower holds contained human cargo, shackled for sale in America. The
African captives below the deck were crammed so closely to each other in spaces
so small that it was impossible for them to stand up or to turn. He recalled the
nauseating stench in the hold and the sound of suffering as many died during
the long voyage across the Atlantic. He remembered how he and other crew
members made captives dance a jig on deck for exercise when they were brought
up for food. He remembered how he, like other crew members, beat
uncooperative captives who refused to eat.

He thought about his time spent on the west coast of Africa working in a
"slave factory" where slavers held Africans in bondage until other traders came
to load them onto ships for export. His mind wandered over memories of
traveling up and down the rivers near Cape Lopez in Africa, buying slaves for
market.

His meandering thoughts brought him back to the water-logged, battered
boat before him, and he wondered why he had been spared from drowning.
Considering his brush with death, he decided, "Prayer kept my spirit alive in the
face of personal danger. Perhaps I do have a spark of faith. I will make daily
prayer a part of my life."

Shortly thereafter, he became the captain of his own slave ship. Trying to
extend his new-found grace to others, he instituted Sunday prayer on the ship. As
he ushered his slaves into the hold of the ship, his heart was moved to give his
captives a bit more room in the lower decks than did other slave ship captains.
He prided himself on the fact that his boat was one of the few slave ships to sail

without losing any slaves to sickness, suicide, or mutiny.

Over time, with prayer, the cold heart of John Newton slowly thawed. His blindness to the cruelty of slave trading slowly lifted. For the first time, he gazed at the weeping, groaning masses of men, women, and children who suffered in his ship's hold and saw how little his favors had meant. He gaped at the chains and shackles. He cringed at the captives' cramped quarters, devoid of light and fresh air. The grotesque sights, which had suddenly come into focus, shocked him. An intense humiliation washed over him like the storm waves in which he had almost drowned.

"Turn the ship around!" ordered John Newton to the amazement of his crew. "We are going back to Africa!" As the ship changed its course, John Newton turned his life around too. He freed his human cargo.

He returned to England and, giving up slave trading, became an ardent abolitionist who worked to stop the slave trade. His influential pamphlet, "Thoughts Upon the African Slave Trade," strongly protested the slavery practices of his time. In 1764, deepening his commitment to personal change, he became a minister for the Church of England.

The obliviousness of his early life, propagating the horror of slavery, became the seed of a hymn he wrote titled "Amazing Grace." Countless people have sung this now popular song celebrating the amazing fact that even a wicked, wretched man can see the evil in his ways, turn his life around, and make a positive change in the world.

Amazing Grace, how sweet the sound,
That saved a wretch like me!
I once was lost, but now am found,
Was blind, but now I see.

'Twas grace that taught my heart to fear,
And grace my fears relieved;
How precious did that grace appear,
The hour I first believed!

Through many dangers, toils, and snares,
I have already come;
'Tis grace has brought me safe thus far,
And grace will lead me home.

When we've been there ten thousand years,
Bright shining as the sun,
We've no less days to sing God's praise,
Than when we'd first begun.

The Prodigal Son

There once was a man who had two grown sons. When the younger son asked for a share of the property, the father divided his estate. The older son stayed and worked hard on the farm, while the younger son took his share, turned it into cash, and set off for a distant country.

The younger son spent his time and money on loose living until, at last, all his wealth was squandered. As a great famine descended upon the land, the younger son was without shelter or food. Pangs of hunger drove him to seek employment. He went to work as a swineherd for a local farmer. Each day as he tossed the pigs their carob pods, he realized that the pigs were better fed than he. He thought, "Even the lowest servants in my father's house have bread to spare."

He decided to return home and beg his father to take him in as a servant. He thought, "I will say that I have sinned against heaven and before my father. I am not worthy to be a son."

As the contrite young man approached his family home, his father saw him at a distance and ran out to greet him. He compassionately threw his arms around the boy and kissed him. The son said, "Father, I am not worthy to be your son. Consider me as a servant. I have sinned before heaven and before you."

But the father called to his servants, "Bring the best robe! Bring shoes fit for a free man, not a servant! Kill the fatted calf, prepare a feast, and make merry! My son was lost, but now he is found!"

The father led his son to a celebration of his return. There was music and dancing and merrymaking.

Meanwhile, the elder son returned home from his work on the family farm and heard the music and dancing. As he approached the house, he asked one of the servants the meaning of the celebration. The servant told him how his father joyously celebrated his younger brother's safe return.

The older brother's face flushed crimson with rage. He refused to go into the house. His father came out to entreat him to join the festivities. The son stubbornly protested, "All these years I have loyally served you, never disobeying your command. You did not give *me* a party! Yet this spendthrift son of yours, who wandered away and squandered the family money on vice and bawdy living, is lavishly celebrated! Why?"

The father smiled warmly at his bristling son and explained, "My celebration of your brother's return takes away none of the love I have for you. Everything I have is already yours! As for all this merrymaking—I delight in the return of my wayward son. It is as if your brother had been dead but came back to life. He was gone, but now he is found. This is indeed a reason to rejoice!"

Fire, Water, Truth, and Falsehood

*L*ong ago, Fire, Water, Truth, and Falsehood lived together in one large house. Although all were polite toward each other, they kept their distance. Truth and Falsehood sat on opposite sides of the room. Fire constantly leapt out of Water's path.

One day they went hunting together. They found a large number of cattle and began driving them home to their village. "Let us share these cattle equally," said Truth as they traveled across the grasslands. "This is the fair way to divide our captives."

No one disagreed with Truth except Falsehood. Falsehood wanted more than an equal share but kept quiet about it for the moment. As the four hunters traveled back to the village, Falsehood went secretly to Water and whispered, "You are more powerful than Fire. Destroy Fire and then there will be more cattle for each of us!"

Water flowed over Fire, bubbling and steaming until Fire was gone. Water meandered along, cheerfully thinking about more cattle for itself.

Falsehood, meanwhile, whispered to Truth. "Look! See for yourself! Water has killed Fire! Let us leave Water, who has cruelly destroyed our warmhearted friend. We must take the cattle high in the mountains to graze."

As Truth and Falsehood traveled up the mountain, Water tried to follow. But the mountain was too steep, and Water could not flow upwards. Water washed down upon itself, splashing and swirling around rocks as it tumbled down the slope. Look and see! Water is still tumbling down the mountainside to this day.

Truth and Falsehood arrived at the mountaintop. Falsehood turned to Truth and said in a loud voice, "I am more powerful than you! You will be my servant. I am your master. All the cattle belong to me!"

Truth rose up and spoke out, "I will not be your servant!"

They battled and battled. Finally they brought the argument to Wind to decide who was master.

Wind didn't know. Wind blew all over the world to ask people whether Truth or Falsehood was more powerful. Some people said, "A single word of Falsehood can completely destroy Truth." Others insisted, "Like a small candle in the dark, Truth can change every situation."

Wind finally returned to the mountain and said, "I have seen that Falsehood is very powerful. But it can rule only where Truth has stopped struggling to be heard."

And it has been that way ever since.

The Red and Blue Coat

CENTRAL AFRICA—CONGO

There once were two childhood friends who were determined to remain close companions always. When they were grown, they each married and built their houses facing one another. Just a small path formed a border between their farms.

One day a trickster from the village decided to test their friendship. He dressed himself in a two-color coat that was divided down the middle, red on the right side and blue on the left side. Wearing this coat, the man walked along the narrow path between the two houses. The two friends were each working opposite each other in their fields. The trickster made enough noise as he traveled between them to cause each friend to look up from his side of the path at the same moment and notice him.

At the end of the day, one friend said to the other, "Wasn't that a beautiful red coat that man was wearing today?"

"No," replied the other. "It was blue."

"I saw that man clearly as he walked between us!" said the first. "His coat was red."

"You are wrong!" the second man said. "I saw it too. It was blue."

"I know what I saw!" insisted the first man. "The coat was red."

"You don't know anything," replied the second angrily. "It was blue!"

"So," shouted the first, "you think I am stupid? I know what I saw. It was red!"

"Blue!" the other man said.

"Red!" "Blue!" "Red!" "Blue!"

They began to beat each other and roll around on the ground.

Just then the trickster returned and faced the two men, who were punching and kicking each other and shouting, "Our friendship is over!"

The trickster walked directly in front of them, displaying his coat. He laughed loudly at their silly fight. The two friends saw that his two-color coat was divided down the middle, blue on the left and red on the right.

The two friends stopped fighting and screamed at the man in the two-colored coat, "We have lived side by side all our lives like brothers! It is all *your* fault that we are fighting! You started a war between us."

"Don't blame me for the battle," replied the trickster. "I did not *make* you fight. *Both* of you are wrong. And *both* of you are right. Yes, what each one said was true! You are fighting because you only looked at my coat from your *own* point of view."

Tongue Meat

EAST-CENTRAL AFRICA—SWAHILI

The sultan's wife was thin and unhappy. Although great riches surrounded her and servants fed her the finest foods, she remained lean and listless. This distressed the sultan, for he did not know how to please her.

It happened that near the sultan's palace there lived a very poor man whose wife was plump and happy. The sultan invited the poor man to visit him and privately asked, "How is it that your wife is so fat, joyous, and healthy? What is the secret of her well-being?"

The poor man replied, "It is no secret! Every day I nourish my happy wife by feeding her *meat of the tongue.*"

"Aha!" cried the sultan, delighted with this simple solution. He immediately ordered his cook to buy the tongue of every animal slaughtered at the market. For days the sultan's wife was given tongue meat prepared in exotic sauces. Although she ate tongue meat several times a day, she still remained thin and sad.

Finally the sultan demanded that the poor man exchange wives with him. Despite protests, the poor man's wife was taken to the palace, and the sultan's thin, sad wife was delivered to the poor man's home.

As soon as the poor man's wife arrived at the palace, she became sad and grew thinner with each passing day. Her happiness and beauty faded like a wilted blossom.

At the poor man's home, meanwhile, the sultan's wife grew happier and began gaining weight. At sunset each night, when the poor man returned from his work, he would tell his royal wife all the funny things that had happened to him that day. He would make her howl with laughter until tears of joy ran down her cheeks. Then he would sing her songs, accompanied by his banjo, until late in the evening, and she would dance. Each night was spent in conversation, song, and story.

During the day, the royal wife would chuckle as she thought about the funny things her new husband had told her the night before. Although her food was simple and the portions quite modest, she grew plump in a short time. Her hair began to shine, and her skin had a healthy glow.

When the sultan saw his old wife and the poor man walking in the marketplace, he wanted her back. She refused to go, saying, "I am much better off with my new husband."

The sultan was amazed at her transformation and in a jealous rage demanded, "What has this poor man given you that I, a great and rich sultan, cannot offer? What has caused such a change in you?"

The wife told the sultan how she and her new husband passed each evening together in story and song. The sultan's eyes filled with understanding, and he left the couple to their happiness. He now humbly knew what the poor man meant when he said that he fed his wife *meat of the tongue.*

Why Wisdom Is Everywhere

WEST AFRICA—ASHANTI

Anansi, the spider, had all the wisdom in the world stored in a huge pot. Nyame, the sky god, had given it to him. Anansi had been instructed to share it with everyone. Anansi looked in the pot every day. He learned how to make things out of fiber, how to hunt and build houses, and how to live well with family and neighbors. The pot was full of wonderful ideas and skills.

Anansi greedily thought, "I will not share this treasure of knowledge with everyone. I will keep all the wisdom for myself!"

Anansi decided to hide the wisdom on top of a tall tree. Holding the pot full of knowledge, he started to climb the tallest tree in the jungle. He struggled to balance the pot in front of himself while climbing at the same time.

Anansi's son, Intikuma, watched with great fascination as his father struggled up the tree. Finally he simply said, "If you tie the pot to your back, it will be easier to cling to the tree and climb."

Anansi heard this sensible advice but shouted in a rage, "A young one with some common sense knows more than I, who has the pot of wisdom!" Anansi threw down the pot of wisdom in a fit of temper and disgust.

Pieces of wisdom flew in every direction. People found bits of wisdom scattered about and took them home for their family and neighbors. That is why to this day, no one person has *all* the world's wisdom. People everywhere share small pieces of it whenever they exchange ideas.

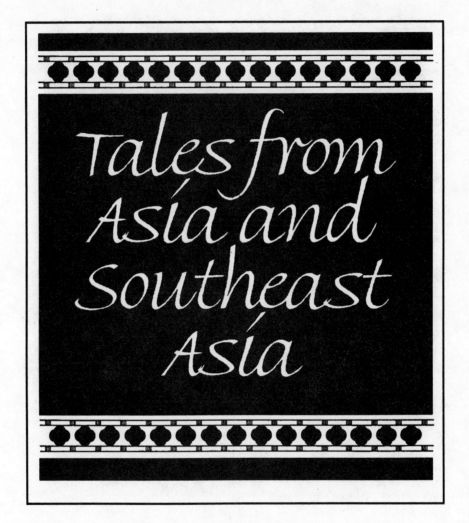

The Parts of the House Argue

A large family once lived together in a nipa palm tree house. One day the people in the house began to quarrel about who was the most important member of the family. Before long the parts of the house began to quarrel too.

The poles that supported the house high off the ground started grumbling. One said, "I am the most important because I was driven into the earth first." The rest replied, "We are all just as important as you because without us you could not do your job of keeping the house off the wet ground."

As the poles quarreled about their importance, the floor supports shouted, "No one would care about the poles if we were not here to connect you!"

The cross supports cried out to the floor supports, "Without us, you would wobble and sag!"

The floor sniped to the cross supports and the floor supports, "Without me, neither of you would have a reason to exist."

The woven bamboo walls chimed in nastily to the floor, "Who would walk on you if we were not here to create rooms?"

The roof beams replied to the walls, "You could not stand up if it were not for our support!"

The bamboo ceiling shouted to the beams, "I hold the walls together!"

The palm-leaf roof chided each part of the house, "I keep the rain from

101

rotting all of you!"

As they argued, they realized that none could win the argument since they were *all* of great use to the house. When with one breath the parts of the house proclaimed, "None is important without the other," the quarreling between the members of the family in the house ceased. Cured of misfortune, the family lived in peace and harmony from that day forward.

The Tiger's Whisker

After many years in battle, a fierce warrior returned home so somber that it seemed to his wife as if his spirit had been killed in battle and that only his flesh and bones walked through the door. Although she welcomed him with great embraces and tears of joy, he did not respond to her touch. His icy eyes did not meet her gaze. He seated himself at the table and stared out the window.

The wife tried to engage him in conversation, but he did not reply. She prepared a huge, tasty meal, which he barely ate. She hovered over him like a mother bird over a new brood and chattered on, telling him jokes and the news of events he had missed in his absence. At night she affectionately curled her arms over his shoulder and smothered his head with kisses. But he turned away and slept with his back to her, pulling the covers tightly around his body.

The wife became distraught at his coldness. She scolded him for being so cruel and hardhearted. "How can you treat me this way!" she wailed. "I have waited so long for your return and suffered in my loneliness!" She dashed out the door and ran until she came to the house of a wise old man who was known to make potions and magical charms.

Tearfully she pleaded, "Please, give me a love potion that will make my husband love me again. He has returned home from war with no love left in his heart."

The old man listened carefully to her complaint and finally replied,

103

"There is a special charm needed in a situation like this. I can help you win back your husband's love, but to make the potion, I will need the whisker of a fierce tiger. If you can bring me such a whisker, I can help you win back your husband's love."

The woman's mouth dropped open, and her eyebrows arched in surprise. "A tiger's whisker!" she exclaimed. "That will be impossible to obtain!"

The old man replied, "If you truly want to win the love of your husband, then you will bring me what I ask."

The woman walked away from the old man's house, deep in thought. Her heart ached. She could not bear the situation as it was, so she went to the market to buy a chunk of meat.

Carrying the meat, she traveled into the jungle until she saw the cave of a tiger. Hiding at a distance, she saw that the huge beast was peacefully asleep in the sun. The woman could not help but notice its sharp claws. She sat as still as a stone and watched the tiger's belly move as he breathed. At last, she left the meat on the spot where she had been sitting and went home.

Each day, the woman returned to the tiger's cave with the meat. Each day, she left the meat a few inches closer and patiently watched the animal. After several weeks, the tiger allowed her to approach and place the meat in front of him. More time passed, and the tiger allowed her to sit beside him as he ate. He would then stretch himself and sleep with his head near her lap. The first time she reached out and touched his sleek fur, a tremble ran through her body. The tiger purred like a giant house cat and slept on.

Many days later, as she sat beside the huge, napping creature, she took tiny scissors from her pocket and carefully snipped a whisker.

She slipped away with the hard-won treasure in her pocket. When she was out of the jungle, she burst into a run that took her all the way to the old man's house. Clutching the tiger's whisker in her hand, she held it up and cried out with joy, "Here it is! I have the tiger's whisker! Now, make me the love potion that will win me back my husband's love."

The old man took the whisker and examined it carefully. "It is truly what you say it is. Tell me, how did you obtain it?"

The woman replied, "I was very patient. I approached the beast carefully and gently, leaving my offerings at a great distance. Each day, I came just a bit closer. After a long time, when I was certain that the creature trusted me, I moved closer still. Finally, I was able to reach out and touch him, for, at long last, he was not afraid."

The old man nodded as the woman unfolded her tale. "That is very interesting," he said, tossing the whisker into the fire.

The woman shrieked with alarm. "After all my effort you have thrown away the special ingredient you need to make the love potion!"

The old man smiled gently and replied, "You do not need a love potion. Any woman who can tame a ferocious tiger can certainly win the love of her husband. Go home, dear woman, and be patient with your husband. Trust that the magic charm to win his heart is already within you."

The woman returned home with new understanding. She stopped scolding. She stopped demanding love. With great patience and the gentle warmth that had tamed a tiger, she melted the icy heart of her warrior husband.

Little Lizard's Sorrow

A rich but greedy gambler devised a clever game to play with other wealthy people. The rules were simple. Each player would bet an item of equal value. The gambler would then challenge his opponents to name something they thought he might not have in his store of possessions. If the gambler could produce the item, he would win and gain whatever objects his opponents had bet.

At first the gambler won by luck, but after many years of playing the game, the gambler acquired such a quantity of things that it was impossible to name anything he did not own. In time, his wealth was vast. He built a huge housing compound and filled even his servants' houses with multitudes of things.

One hot day a beggar knocked at the gambler's gate. The gatekeeper opened the door and saw a man dressed in crude rags holding a begging bowl made out of a coconut shell. "I have come, like the others, to challenge the gambler at his game," the beggar said.

The servant rushed to tell the gambler that there was a man at the gate who wanted to wager. The eyes of the gambler, who was always ready to play, brightened. "Hurry and bring the man inside!" he ordered.

When the gambler saw the beggar, he laughed. "In order to play with me, you must have something with which to bet. You are a poor man. What have you brought?"

"I have brought everything I own," replied the beggar.

"Ha!" said the gambler scornfully. "You have brought just a begging bowl!"

"Not so!" the beggar replied. "I have brought *myself* to wager, for that is all I truly own."

The gambler was puzzled and said, "Let me be clear. If I win, you would become my slave?"

"Exactly," said the beggar. "But to be fair, you must match my bet. I dare you to wager everything you believe *yourself* to own."

The gambler laughed at such a proposal. "I own vast quantities of goods!" he shouted.

Yet the thrill of such a wager tempted him. He thought to himself, "I own an endless array of items. This fool of a beggar could not possibly name something I do not have in storage. Of course I will win and gain something new—a slave."

"Yes," said the gambler with a wicked grin, "I agree to the wager. Now go ahead. To win, you must name something I do not have! I dare you to try."

"I must think carefully," said the beggar. "There is much at stake." The beggar considered for a long time and finally said, "Do you have a chipped cup?"

The gambler exclaimed, "A chipped cup? Why, of course! I have thousands of cups, of every color, size, and shape! Surely there is a chipped cup!"

The gambler's servants searched every cupboard, but since the gambler was a rich man, he threw away chipped cups. "If one of my servants has a chipped cup, that will count for this wager!" he blustered. But the servants served a rich man, and so they thought themselves rich too. If they had a chipped cup, they also would have thrown it away. There was no chipped cup to be found!

The gambler cried out in disbelief, "Oh no, I have lost the wager!"

The beggar replied, "Do not despair. You have lost only what you believe yourself to own—your possessions. Now they are mine to do with as I please."

Throwing open the doors of the compound, the beggar invited the poor of the city to help themselves to everything they could carry. The gambler wept as he watched a lifetime of riches and winnings leave his house in the hands of the poor. When the house was totally empty of things, the beggar walked away down the road with just his begging bowl in hand. He had taken all that he believed he owned, which was *himself*.

The gambler, meanwhile, could not fathom his bad luck and miserably shook his head, saying, "Tsk, tsk, tsk! How could this happen? Tsk, tsk, tsk! How could this be?"

The gambler shrank

and

shrank

and

shrank

until he became a tiny lizard who still nervously scurries up and down the walls in certain parts of Southeast Asia. People say he makes the sorrowful "tsk, tsk, tsk" sound because he is eternally fretting about his lost possessions.

Tales from Europe

The Three Wishes

A poor woodcutter set out one fine morning to cut firewood to sell at the market. "Wish me luck, dear wife," he said, "that I might find some fallen tree in the king's forest. Only the fallen wood is free to poor peasants like ourselves."

As he marched into the forest with his sharp ax over his shoulder, he eyed the trees right and left. All were upright and healthy. Others had come before and scoured the ground of branches. "I'll get some wood by hook or by crook," he muttered. Finally, he stopped in front of a great oak tree. Leafy branches crowned its huge trunk. "Now here is a tree worth its weight in gold!" exclaimed the woodcutter. "I will make a fortune cutting it down for market!"

As he swung his ax high over his shoulder, a tree fairy appeared before him and said, "Stop! Spare this tree, for it has lived longer than you. Respect your elders!"

"But this tree is worth a great amount of money!" protested the woodcutter. "I am tired of laboring so hard, traveling to find broken branches to sell. This is good, hard wood, and I mean to make use of it!"

The fairy threw her arms around the tree and said, "If you give me your word that you will not cut down this ancient tree, I will grant you three wishes."

The woodcutter put down the ax and considered the proposal. "Three wishes?" he mused, thinking about vast wealth.

"If you promise that you will never cut down an old tree, the three wishes

111

will be yours," said the fairy.

"Very well," the woodcutter said. "A promise is a promise. I agree never to cut down an old tree. Besides, I will have no further need to cut wood. I will wish for wealth enough to retire!"

In a twinkling, the woodcutter's ax disappeared, and the fairy vanished. By these signs, the woodcutter knew that the fairy would grant his wishes. He ran home to tell his good wife.

Red-faced and panting, he burst in through the door. "Wife! Wife!" he cried. "We are rich beyond our wildest dreams!"

The wife blinked in disbelief. "How is it that you left this morning despairing of our poverty and you return tonight exclaiming our wealth?"

"I spared a tree in the king's forest," the woodcutter explained, "and a tree fairy said she would grant me three wishes for my kindness!"

"Then think carefully," said the good wife with glee.

"Well then," said the woodcutter, "I might wish for a fine house with a garden."

"Fool!" said the wife. "Think bigger! Wish for a palace!"

"What good is a palace without gold enough to maintain it with servants, cooks, and stable boys?" said the woodcutter. "I must wish for a bag of gold."

"You are not thinking big enough, Husband! Why wish for a bag of gold when you could have a cartload of it?"

"And a fine horse to pull the cart!" the woodcutter exclaimed.

"Don't waste your wishes!" cried the woman. "You could have a herd of horses!"

"All this thinking," said the woodcutter, "is making me very hungry. I wish we had some sausage."

In a blink, a huge chain of sausages fell into the middle of the room. "Oh no!" screeched the wife. "You've wasted a wish! What a fool you are. You could have had anything, and you think about your stomach!"

Unable to stand the tirade of his wife, the woodcutter said, "Oh, I wish those sausages were stuck to your nose!"

In as little time as it takes to tell it, the sausages stuck fast to the wife's nose. Horrified, the couple tried to pull them off. The harder they pulled, the tighter they stuck. The wife fell to the floor sobbing so miserably that her husband said, "Well, I suppose there's nothing to do but to wish the sausages were off."

In a blink, the sausages were on a plate on the table. The woodcutter and his wife could do nothing but laugh at their own folly. Nothing good ever comes from arguing, they agreed. "At least we have a fine supper," the woodcutter said. And never a finer supper was shared.

The Wooden Bowl

There was a celebration on the day that the old man came to live on the small farm owned by his son and his son's young wife. A fine meal of freshly grown vegetables and home-baked bread was set out on the table. The couple covered a new bed in a small adjoining room with a warm cover and soft pillow. "We hope you will be comfortable here," said the son as he carried his father's few belongings into the room.

"As long as I have family around me," the old man said, wiping a tear from his eye, "I will be happy. Perhaps there is still enough strength in these old limbs to help a bit on your farm. I want to be useful."

"You are welcome to work as you will or rest when you want, Father," said the son.

The next morning, the old man dressed himself in work clothes and went out to the barn to feed the pigs and chickens. He scooped the chicken feed into a wooden bowl and scattered it about the yard. He watched with amusement as the rooster strutted. "Oh, to be young again," he sighed to himself as he rubbed his stiff hands to subdue the pain he felt in his old joints.

Each day the old man did as much as his body would allow, and each night he sat with his son and his son's wife at dinner. He noticed the swelling of his daughter-in-law's belly and eagerly looked forward to the day when his first grandchild would be born.

Days melted into months and, finally, the child arrived. The old man held his grandson with great tenderness. He recalled his own son's small face as he gazed with wonder at the tiny eyes that stared back at him.

"Be careful how you hold him," said the young wife. "Your hands are trembling."

The old man had noticed it too. The dull pain he felt in his joints had increased each day, and now his hands were betraying him.

"Don't drop him," exclaimed the wife, who worriedly snatched the child away.

After that, the old man's changes came quickly. By the time the small boy could sit up by himself, the old man found it harder to cast the chicken feed from the feeding bowl. His hands could not grip a pitchfork. His son tried to ignore his father's aging.

By the time the grandson could walk, the old man could not stride any longer into the barn. His steps were slow. His back was beginning to stoop. He worked as he could but did not accomplish much. Times were hard and the son had to let most of the farm help go. Now he worked from early hours to sunset along with his wife. The old man tended the little boy but could hardly keep up with him.

One night after a grueling day in the fields, the son and his tired wife sat down to a hastily prepared dinner. The boy sat next to his grandpa as the wife placed a large bowl of porridge on the table. "Times have been better," she sighed. "I am looking forward to the first fresh vegetable crops."

Grandpa tried to ladle some porridge. His hand shook so much that he toppled the bowl onto the dusty floor. "How clumsy!" the wife shouted.

It was more than the old man could bear. He slowly got up and left the table. His son ignored the problem and sat silently as his grumbling wife cleaned up the mess.

Each day the old man's condition worsened. He began to drool. The wife sat him at a small table in the corner, away from the family as they ate.

One night the old man's trembling hand knocked his porcelain eating bowl off his little table. It landed with a crash and broke on the floor. The wife went out to the barn and got the wooden bowl used for chicken feed. She filled it with food and served the old man another supper. "Now here is one you won't break," she said. Her husband stared into the distance and again said nothing.

One day when the young child was older and had learned to speak, his father and mother found him industriously chipping away with a stone at two chunks of wood. "What are you doing?" the boy's father asked. His son replied, "I am making you each a present!"

"What could it be?" his father asked with delight.

"I am making the wooden chicken-feed bowls I will give you and Mama to eat from when you are old," said the boy.

The boy's words stunned his father. The future loomed before him, and he saw himself old and forgotten.

When his vision cleared, he noticed his frail father sitting alone in the corner. He gathered the old man in his arms and led him to the table and set a place for him with their best dishes. That night as the young boy watched, his father fed the old grandpa tenderly with a silver spoon. He handed his wife a cloth napkin, and she gently wiped the old man's drooling lips.

From that day on, they both treated the old man with the same kindness and respect they hoped to receive from their own son in their elderly years.

Treat the old with love that is ample.
The very best teacher is a good example.

The Happy Man's Shirt

The king's son was so sad that his eyes forever threatened a downpour of tears. In the palace, servants catered to his every need. The cooks prepared the tastiest dishes for him. Toy makers created the cleverest playthings. Tutors shared their most stimulating ideas. Yet he remained sullen and sad.

The king cherished the boy and wished only for his happiness. Finally, unable to bear the prince's despair a moment longer, the king called for advisers from far and wide to study the situation and provide a solution to the prince's sorrow. After much stargazing, consideration, and calculation, the wise counselors decreed, "You must dress the prince in the shirt of a truly happy man, and he will be cured of his sorrow."

Delighted with this simple solution, the king set out on a journey to find a truly happy man whose shirt would make his son happy again. With a great retinue he traveled to a nearby town where there lived a pious priest whose radiant smile cheered and comforted the heart of everyone he met. Because the priest was known to be a happy man, the king went directly to his home. The priest greeted the king with a humble bow. "To what do I owe this honor, Your Majesty?" asked the priest.

The king replied, "Since you are so revered for your holiness and good nature, I would like to know if you would accept the position of bishop, should it be offered to you?"

The priest smiled happily and replied, "Most certainly!"

The king frowned and said to himself with a sigh, "This man's shirt will not do. He is not truly happy. If he were truly happy, he would want no more than what he already has."

The king journeyed on to another land where lived a sultan whose kingdom was peaceful and whose people were content. The visiting king was welcomed with a royal feast. At the dinner, the visiting king said to the sultan, "You seem to be a happy man. What makes you so?"

The sultan replied, "I have everything I could possibly want and truly want no more. Yet late at night as I fall asleep, I worry about losing all I have worked so hard to gain."

Once again the king sighed and said to himself, "This man's shirt will not do."

In place after place, the king searched but could not find a man who was truly content with his life.

The king was about to give up the quest when he happened to be riding across a vineyard and heard the most joyous singing. In the distance he saw a poor farmer who was harvesting his grapes and singing at the top of his lungs in a voice that rivaled the birds. The king approached the peasant, who turned with a sunny smile and said, "Good day!"

The king climbed down off his horse and walked toward the man. "You seem so happy today," said the king.

The man replied, "Indeed I am, every day. I am blessed with a wonderful life!"

The king said, "Your smile is so radiant. Come with me to the royal castle. You will be surrounded with luxury and never want for anything again."

The man munched a grape and said, "No, thank you. I would not give up my life for all the castles in the world."

The king could not contain his joy. "My son is saved! My son is saved!" he shouted. "Please, you must do something for your king!"

The man bowed and said, "Anything you wish, Your Majesty."

The king reached out and, opening the farmer's ragged jacket, shouted,

"You must give me your shirt!"

The king's eyes stared wide with astonishment at the sight of the young man's muscular chest. The truly happy man was not wearing a shirt.

The Dancing Lass of Anglesey

Listen, my friends, to a tale of the time when battles were fought, and yet none would be killed! The victor was chosen by dancer's skill and not by the measure of most blood spilled.

In Scotland long ago, a king was ashen pale with fright.
He trembled to think that fifteen men would claim his lands that night.
They were coming to dance his lands away,
with pounding steps and graceful sway.
Each was a dancing champion with steps so firm and strong
that none of the king's own champions could dance as fine or long.

"I'll lose my gold. I'll lose my lands,"
the king worried and wrung his hands.
"I cannot gain the victory
unless I find the lass from Anglesey.
None can dance as well as she."

He sent north and south and east and west
to find the one who danced the best.
"Go forth, my Lords, and bring to me
The Dancing Lass of Anglesey.

120

They say she dances the time away
till flowers bloom and wheat crops sway,
till everything dies and fades away,
till nothing can stand anymore.

She dances the seasons,
she dances the time,
she dances the tides,
the ageless rhyme.
With delicate feet she keeps the beat
till none can stand anymore.
She'll dance them to the floor."

Well ... they found her on a distant hill and brought her before the king.
"If you'll dance for me," he said, "I'll give you anything.
I'll give you a mill and lands," he said,
"and my bonniest knight for you to wed."

She replied, "I'll take your mill.
I'll take your land.
I care not for a knight to take my hand.
So keep your bonny boy ... I'll dance just for the joy."

And so came them all
to the great king's hall,
and she danced them
one by one.

With delicate feet she kept the beat
till none could stand anymore.
She stepped, she twirled in a dancer's world,
till they lay in a heap on the floor.

When the fifteen knights were all undone,
she danced the king's men one by one.
And then she took the king
and danced him to the floor.
She leapt about the heap of men,
who could not fight anymore.

So she gathered their swords and their silver buckles
and out the door went she.
For none could dance as long or strong
as the lass from Anglesey,
the Dancing Lass from Anglesey.

Oh, I wish that it were in modern times
a battle could be fought, and yet none would be killed.
The champion would be chosen by dancer's skill,
and not by the measure of most blood spilled.

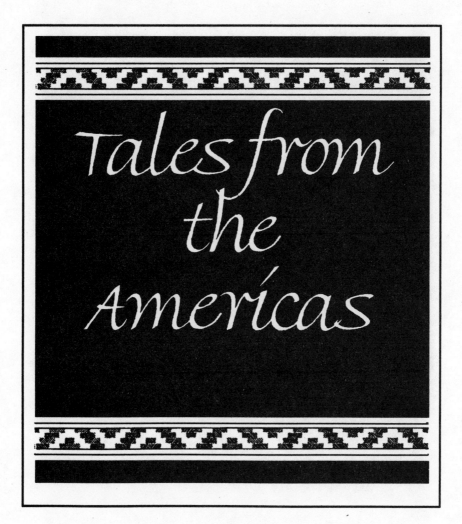

Tales from the Americas

How War Was Ended

NORTH AMERICAN ARCTIC—CENTRAL YUP'IK ESKIMO

*F*ive hundred years before the first outsiders came to central Alaska, there lived a powerful Yup'ik warrior named Apanugpak. He was renowned by the Yup'ik people for his skill with the harpoon and bow and arrow.

It was a time of great madness and terror among the Yup'ik. Warring groups attacked each other across the tundra. People lived in fear within their subterranean sod houses, unable to safely light fires or to cook food. Each band of warriors had a "smeller" who traveled with them. The "smellers" had such keen noses they could sense even one particle of smoke in the pristine air of the cold tundra and direct the warriors to the source of the fire. People were cold, hungry, and afraid.

It came to pass that one day Apanugpak had a vision. In the vision he saw houses in villages everywhere vanishing into the sky as curling wisps of black smoke. He saw a crimson lake of blood, made from the dripping wounds of slain warriors. As he gazed at these strange sights, Apanugpak, the bravest of warriors, was struck with terror. He trembled as he watched the ghosts of dead warriors slowly rise up to do battle with the living.

At that moment, Apanugpak knew that war was futile. No side could win, for as warriors killed more and more people, the vast army of ghosts would continue to increase. Like memories of horror driving people to revenge, the ghosts of war would vanquish the living and cause great suffering to continue endlessly. Apanugpak knew then that war must end.

He was the most respected of all the fierce warriors. People were surprised when he held up his harpoon and his bow and arrows and said, "These things were created to help us hunt for food, not to cause death to each other. I will not use these tools to fight people any longer." When Apanugpak, the greatest warrior, put down his weapons, all the others followed. The time of madness was over. The killing was finished.

Discord between people found a different expression. People created new kinds of contests. Instead of killing each other in battle, warring bands began to compete energetically with each other in singing contests, dancing contests, and insulting contests. Colorful gatherings rich in music, movement, and pointed, clever words settled disputes.

Peace prevailed and people were able to light their hearth fires again. The sweet smell of savory food, cooking in subterranean homes, signaled the return of sanity to the land of ice and cold.

How the Quetzal Got Its Red Breast

CENTRAL AMERICA—MAYA

*L*ong ago in the Sierra de las Minas, a mountain range in Guatemala, the quetzal, an ancient sacred bird, flew though the lush rain forest. The quetzal protected Maya chieftains in battle, hovering over them with iridescent green plumage spread like a soaring shield.

In 1524, a Spaniard named Pedro de Alvarado marched with his army into Guatemala. Alvarado found the Maya world rich with art, science, and majesty. Even at that time, the Mayas were an old culture. The ancients had created great pyramids and an accurate calendar. Their ornate written language, carved in stone, revealed a knowledge of complex mathematics and astronomy.

Pedro de Alvarado was not interested in these wonders, for he had come to conquer the Mayas and capture their gold. Arriving at the highland city of Quezaltenango, the red-haired Spaniard led a violent attack. Spanish conquistadors with shining armor, swords, and guns fought the Mayas, who vainly sought to protect themselves with wicker shields, clubs, and spears.

Alvarado himself battled the Maya chief Tecún Umán. Umán's protector bird, the quetzal, flew above the bloody skirmish, darting this way and that as the clubs and swords swung and lunged. At the moment that Alvarado's lance pierced the Maya chief's breast, the quetzal fell to the earth. Its emerald green plumage shrouded Umán's lifeless body.

At dawn, the quetzal rose and flew up off Umán's body. Its radiant green breast feathers had turned crimson, stained with the blood of the fallen Maya chief. From that moment on, the breast feathers of all quetzals have been blood red.

Quetzals still fly in the endangered rain forests of Guatemala. Their long, green tail feathers and deep red breasts make them a sought-after sight by naturalists. Artists have pictured the quetzal in patterns woven into Guatemalan textiles. Modern hands exchange Guatemalan money bearing their name, and official medals and emblems carry their image.

But their emerald green breast feathers are no more. The crimson stain of native blood, spilled by conquistadors long ago, is on display as the ancient, sacred quetzal flies over its disappearing forest habitat.

Old Dog and Coyote

A long time ago in the Mexican desert, there was an old dog who lived with a chicken farmer. One day the farmer found the old dog fast asleep while the chickens cackled and raised a ruckus at a wolf prowling outside their yard. The farmer chased the wolf away and raged at the dog, "Wake up, you lazy creature! You are a useless watchdog! Go and find your own food today!"

Hungry and humiliated, the old dog crept from the farmer's shack into the desert. He poked about the cactus and yucca plants for small rodents and lizards to catch and eat. A howl made him look across the desert, and there he saw Coyote jumping up and down. Curious, the old dog padded over and snarled, "What are you doing?"

Coyote replied, "Do not bother me. I am practicing for my big jump."

The old dog was confused and asked, "Where are you going to jump?"

Coyote bragged, "I am the best jumper in the desert. I am going to jump over a giant cactus."

"You are foolish!" the old dog said. "You cannot jump over a cactus!"

Coyote replied, "Anything is possible with practice. Watch me try."

Before them stood a huge, prickly-thorned cactus. Coyote took a great, running leap and, soaring to the top of the cactus, landed directly on top of the thorns. The old dog had never heard a howl as loud as the one Coyote made as he tumbled to the ground, stuck all over with prickly thorns.

The old dog felt sorry for Coyote's pitiful condition and said, "I cannot bear to see you in such pain. Let me help."

The old dog spent the next few hours gently pulling out the thorns, both big and small, with his teeth. When he was finished, Coyote rolled over and sighed, "Ahhh! What a fine dog you are!"

The old dog groaned with hunger and said, "No, I am not. I am a useless old watchdog. I cannot guard the chickens. No one is afraid of me. See, even *you* do not run away. Now the farmer will not feed me anymore."

Coyote's eyes brightened. "I am your wild dog brother. I will return your kindness to me."

Coyote whispered a plan into the old dog's ear.

That night the old dog returned to the farmer's chicken yard. Coyote crept among the chickens and stirred up such a racket of cackling that the farmer woke up to investigate the noise. He arrived to see the old dog growling and chasing Coyote, who ran with his tail between his legs.

"Good dog!" exclaimed the farmer. "So I see you are not useless after all! Tomorrow I will give you a fine bone!"

Coyote ran to the top of a small hill and howled with laughter.

Every few nights from then on, Coyote made great sport of waking the farmer by stirring up the chickens and pretending to be frightened of the dog. As for the old watch dog, the farmer believed what was useful to him and fed the dog generously until the day he died.

Paca and Beetle

 green and gold parrot watched a small brown beetle crawl along the endless riverbank.

"Good morning," squawked the parrot. "Where are you going?"

"I am on a long journey," replied the beetle.

Just then, a paca, a small rat-like creature, ran by. The swift-footed paca dashed circles around the beetle and laughed. "You are going on a journey? You crawl so slowly that it will take your entire life to reach your destination! If you could move as I do, you would be more likely to accomplish something. Look at how fast I can run!"

Paca demonstrated his speed by darting to and fro. "You will never get anywhere!" he mocked. "You are too slow!"

The brown beetle ignored the paca's insulting words and kept creeping along.

The parrot looked down at the two and said, "Paca, your words are boastful but not necessarily true. Beetle is slow, but he gets where he wants to be. Perhaps the two of you would like to have a race. Each of you go to the tree around the river bend as fast as you are able. I will give whoever gets there first a new coat as a prize."

Paca said, "Surely with my speed I will win! I would choose a fine yellow coat with black spots like the jaguar. That would be a fitting replacement for my brown and white fur."

131

Beetle replied, "I agree to the race, and if I win, I want a coat just like yours, my wise parrot friend."

"Very well," said the parrot. "Go as fast as you can!"

Paca dashed off along the riverbank. "Oh, I shall have a long tail too!" he shouted as he sped away. Suddenly he stopped, breathless, and said to himself, "Why rush? The beetle won't arrive for hours!" He walked the riverbank at a comfortable pace, thinking about his beautiful new fur.

When he arrived at the tree, a small voice said, "What took you so long, my friend?"

Paca's eyes grew wide at the sight of the little brown beetle.

"How did you get here so quickly?" asked the paca.

"I flew," the beetle replied.

"You flew?" screamed the paca. "I didn't know you could fly! You cheated!"

The parrot interrupted, "Beetle did not cheat! I told you both to go as swiftly as you could. Beetle won the race fairly. Just because you were unaware of Beetle's hidden talent doesn't mean that he shouldn't have flown to win. Beetle does not brag about flying. He keeps his wings modestly folded and uses them only when necessary."

Paca grumbled and went away wearing his plain brown and white color. Meanwhile, the little beetle's back began to shine, for all time, a bright green like the wing feathers of the parrot. Tiny golden spots, the color of the parrot's head, twinkled all over his shell.

Gluscabi and the
Magic Game Bag

NORTH AMERICAN EASTERN WOODLANDS—ABENAKI

G luscabi walked quietly through the pine forest, his bow and arrow poised to shoot a small animal for dinner. Although his moccasins made no sound, the animals sensed his coming and hid silently in the woods. Gluscabi searched everywhere but could not find any animals to hunt.

"Hunting takes too long!" said Gluscabi. He strode directly to Grandmother Woodchuck's wigwam beside the river.

Gluscabi lay down on his bedding and began to sing, "I wish I had a game bag to make hunting easier."

Grandmother Woodchuck heard Gluscabi singing and wove some deer hair into a fine, strong bag in which to keep his catch. She tossed it to him, but Gluscabi kept singing.

Grandmother Woodchuck took moose hair and wove an even larger bag for Gluscabi. "Here is your bag," she said, tossing it to him and hoping that he would be pleased.

But Gluscabi kept singing.

Grandmother Woodchuck finally plucked the hairs from her own belly and made a magical game bag that could keep stretching larger and larger.

Gluscabi was very pleased when he received the magical bag. He set out at once for the forest. As he walked through the trees, Gluscabi shouted, "Animals everywhere! Hear my words and listen to my warning! The world is going to be destroyed! All of you will perish! I have come here to help you."

Slowly, anxious animals crept into the clearing and moved toward Gluscabi. "How will you help us?" they all asked.

Gluscabi held up his game bag and proclaimed, "This is a magic bag! If you will climb into it, you will not see the world end."

One by one, all the animals hurried to the bag and climbed inside as Gluscabi held it wide open. Rabbits, muskrats, porcupines, deer, raccoons, squirrels, and bears came in great numbers. The bag continued to stretch. Moose, sables, and partridges arrived. More and more animals came and climbed into the bag until all the animals were there. Gluscabi closed the bag, tied it, and ran all the way home. He shouted with joy, "I will never have to hunt again!"

Grandmother Woodchuck came out of the wigwam to greet him. "Why are you shouting?" she asked.

"Look, Grandmother!" cried Gluscabi excitedly. "Look what I have done! I was clever enough to trick all the animals into climbing in this bag. Now whenever we want some meat to eat, we can just reach into the bag and take some out."

Grandmother Woodchuck looked into the bag and saw that what Gluscabi said was true. The forest was silent as stone, for all the animals in the world were in the magic game bag.

Grandmother Woodchuck was not pleased. "Gluscabi, the animals cannot live in this game bag without food, water, and air. They will soon die, and then there will be no animals left. Is a world without animals the gift you would give to those who will live after you are gone?"

Gluscabi thought about the silent forest. He shook his head and said, "No, I want my children's children's children to live with the animals too. But it is hard work to hunt for food."

Grandmother Woodchuck said, "The hard work will make you clever and strong. The animals must become wiser, too, in order to escape your arrows and traps. There will be a good balance this way."

Gluscabi agreed. He took the magic game bag back to the forest and opened it. He shouted into the bag, "The danger is over! It is safe to come out now!"

All the animals climbed out of the bag and scattered through the forest. To this day in certain places, you can see rabbits, raccoons, wolverines, deer, bears, and many other animals too. They are still here on the earth, everywhere, because Gluscabi listened to the wise advice of Grandmother Woodchuck and did not lazily try to make life easy by hoarding all the animals for himself.

Proverbs from Around the World

Proverbs are the essence of wisdom tales without the storyline. This evocative form of folklore sometimes stands in the stead of a wisdom tale. A thought-provoking proverb can suggest a larger scenario. I invite readers to look at proverbs creatively and imagine the story each proverb suggests.

Shrouds are made without pockets. (Yiddish)

One finger cannot lift a pebble. (Iran)

When elephants battle, the ants perish. (Cambodia)

If you chase two hares, you will not catch either. (Russia)

The pot calls the kettle black. (United States)

The sieve says to the needle: You have a hole in your tail. (Pakistan)

It is better to turn back than to get lost. (Russia)

Handsome words don't butter cabbage. (Germany)

Talk does not cook rice. (China)

After the rain, there is no need for an umbrella. (Bulgaria)

When the kettle boils over, it overflows its own sides. (Yiddish)

You can't chew with somebody else's teeth. (Yiddish)

Mistrust is an ax at the tree of love. (Russia)

If a farmer becomes a king, he will still carry a basket on his back. (Hebrew)

Not all that is black is charcoal. (Philippines)

Little brooks make great rivers. (France)

Every kind of animal can be tamed, but not the tongue of man. (Philippines)

Do not look for apples under a poplar tree. (Slovakia)

Every ass loves to hear himself bray. (England)

He that goes barefoot must not plant thorns. (England)

Better to be a free bird than a captive king. (Denmark)

A blow passes on; a spoken word lingers. (Yiddish)

You can't spit on my back and make me think it's rain. (Yiddish)

A book gives knowledge, but it is life that gives understanding. (Hebrew)

A crooked branch has a crooked shadow. (Japan)

Better bread with water than cake with trouble. (Russia)

The heaviest burden is an empty pocket. (Yiddish)

A candle lights others but consumes itself. (England)

It takes a village to raise a child. (Africa)

The only hungry Mbuti is a lazy Mbuti. (Africa—Pygmy)

It is one thing to cackle and another to lay an egg. (Ecuador)

One dog barks because it sees something; a hundred dogs bark because they
    heard the first dog bark. (China)

To hide one lie, a thousand lies are needed. (India)

A needle wrapped in a rag will be found in the end. (Vietnam)

Do not seek to escape from the flood by clinging to a tiger's tail. (China)

Step by step, one ascends the staircase. (Turkey)

Little by little, the cotton thread becomes a loincloth. (Africa—Dahomey)

Anger is a bad adviser. (Hungary)

Eggs must not quarrel with stones. (Jamaica)

Eyes can see everything except themselves. (Serbo-Croatian)

Haste makes waste. (England)

Every hill has its valley. (Italy)

The highest wisdom is kindness. (Yiddish)

Notes and Bibliography

EPIGRAPH: NAKED TRUTH AND PARABLE

Jacob Kranz, otherwise known as the Maggid of Dubno, was an eighteenth-century Hasidic rabbi who went from town to town in Jewish communities in Eastern Europe telling stories. Once someone asked him why parables could be so powerful and have such a persuasive effect on people. He responded by telling this story about truth and parable.

My retelling, in poetry, is inspired by a prose version of the tale titled "Truth in Gay Clothes," which appears in *A Treasury of Jewish Folklore* by Nathan Ausubel (New York: Crown Publishers, 1948). Another version can be found in *The Maggid of Dubno and His Parables* by Benno Heineman (Spring Valley, N.Y.: Feldheim Publishers, 1978).

TALES FROM ANCIENT INDIA
Jataka Tales

THE TALKATIVE TURTLE

THE WISE MASTER

A FLOCK OF BIRDS

The Jataka tales are ancient fables and stories attributed to Siddhartha Gautama, the Buddha, a Sanskrit word that means "Enlightened One" or "Awakened One." The Buddha was a teacher of spiritual attainment who lived in India between 563 and 483 B.C.E. Some of these oral tales were ancient at the time that the Buddha lived. Jatakas were told to illustrate concepts such as compassion, a reverence for all life, and an understanding of karma, or the laws of cause and effect. Buddhists consider Jataka tales to be stories of the Buddha's remembered births in different forms.

Scholars have long speculated upon how the ancient fables of India mingled with the stories of the West. It is thought that soldiers brought Jataka tales westward after Alexander the Great and his army invaded India in 325 B.C.E At that time, traveling Greeks translated some of the tales into their language. The Hebrew fabulist Rabbi Meir, who lived in Hellenistic Asia Minor during the second century C.E., translated over three hundred fables. From there, thirty of the tales filtered into the Hebrew Talmud and Midrash. Christian crusaders during the eleventh and twelfth centuries brought Arabic versions of the stories back to Europe. Many Jataka tales were inaccurately attributed to Aesop by later writers of the Middle Ages.

As a story genre, fables feature animals who talk and act, wisely and unwisely, like people. As such, they poignantly comment on social behavior. Sometimes dreadful results come to foolish characters because of their actions. Their unfortunate experience points the way to wiser conduct.

Other printed versions of "The Talkative Turtle" can be found in *The Fables of India* by Joseph Gaer (Boston: Little, Brown & Co., 1955) and as "The Turtle Who Talked Too Much" in *Jataka Tales: Fables from the Buddha* by Nancy DeRoin (Boston: Houghton Mifflin Co., 1975).

Another version of "The Wise Master" can be found in *Twenty Jataka Tales* by Noor Inayat Khan (London: George G. Harrap and Co., 1939).

Other versions of "A Flock of Birds" can be found as "Cooperation" in *Jataka Tales: Fables from the Buddha* by DeRoin and as "The Wise Quail" in *The Hungry Tigress: Buddhist Legends and Jataka Tales* by Rafe Martin (Berkeley, Calif.: Parallax Press, 1990).

Tales from The Panchatantra

THE LION MAKERS

THE BLUE JACKAL WHO SHOWED HIS TRUE COLORS

THE LION AND THE RABBIT

The Panchatantra, or "five books," was created, scholars propose, around 200 B.C.E. in Kashmir as a *niti*, or "textbook for wise conduct." Like *The Thousand and One Nights*, *The Panchatantra* has a frame story that contains many interior tales. An ancient king, despairing of the poor conduct of his two sons, engaged a wise Brahman, Vishnusharman, to teach them. The Brahman used moralistic fables and quotes from earlier Hindu Vedas, or scriptures, to teach the princes to value and preserve friendships and to exercise their intelligence. This collection of ancient fables incorporates several older Hindu stories and Jataka tales. It is one of the most widely translated books in the world. An English translation of the total text can be found in *The Panchatantra, Translated from the Sanskrit* by Arthur W. Ryder (Chicago: University of Chicago Press, 1956).

Versions of the three tales from *The Panchatantra* included in this anthology can be found in Ryder's translation. *The Blue Jackal* has been presented in picture book form by Marcia Brown (New York: Scribner, 1977) and by Mehlli Gobhai (Englewood Cliffs, N.J.: Prentice Hall, 1968). Other versions of "The Lion and the Rabbit" are included in:

Fables of India by Joseph Gaer (Boston: Little Brown & Co., 1955).
Kalila and Dimna: Selected Fables of Bidpai by Ramsey Wood (New York: Alfred A. Knopf, 1980).
Joining In: An Anthology of Audience Participation Stories by Teresa Miller (Boston: Yellow Moon Press, 1988).

The Blind Men and the Elephant (India)

My retelling of this tale, which is widely told in India, is inspired by Jalal Al-din Rumi's version in his volume of poetry titled the *Masnavi* (couplets of inner meaning). Rumi was a Persian mystic and poet whose twenty-five-thousand-line book is an encyclopedia of Sufi lore. It also includes many fables from older collections, such as the animal tales attributed to both Aesop of ancient Greece and Bidpai of India. In one poem from the volume, Rumi uses the elephant as a metaphor for spiritual understanding, humorously commenting on the difficulty of complete comprehension while investigating only a small aspect of the whole. A translation of Rumi's couplets on the subject of the elephant can be found in *An Introduction to Persian Literature* by Reuben Levy (New York: Columbia University Press, 1969).

Children's picture book versions of this folktale include *Seven Blind Mice* by Ed Young (New York: Philomel, 1992) and *The Blind Men and the Elephant: An Old Tale from India* by Lillian Fox Quigley (New York: Scribner, 1956).

TALES FROM CHINA
Taoist Parables

BLINDED BY GREED (LIEH TZU)

THE STOLEN AX (LIEH TZU)

THE BEST FIT (HAN FEI)

THE POWERFUL FIGHTING COCK (CHUANG TZU)

WHOSE DREAM IS THIS? (CHUANG TZU)

THE USELESS TREE (CHUANG TZU)

A FARMER'S HORSE RAN OFF (LIU AN)

The stories retold in this section are based on parables by authors who were influenced by the writing of the philosopher Lao Tzu. Born about 570 B.C.E., Lao Tzu wrote a monumental work titled the *Tao Teh Ching*. This mystical philosophical work expounds the wisdom of the Tao, or "the Way," which values simplicity, humility, and calm and celebrates the intelligence that can be gained by observing the workings of the natural world. Later writers Chuang Tzu and Lieh Tzu, who lived around 300 B.C.E., and Han Fei, a writer who lived shortly after, drew upon the profound philosophy in the *Tao Teh Ching* to create colorful, anecdotal tales that illustrated the values and ideas in the book. Their poetic parables were a vivid contrast to the practical legalism of the Confucianism that prevailed during their day.

Other versions of Chuang Tzu stories can be found in *The Way of Chuang Tzu* by Thomas Merton (New York: New Directions Publishing, 1965) and in *The Wisdom of*

China and India, edited by Lin Yutang (New York: The Modern Library, Random House, 1942).

Versions of Lieh Tzu's and Han Fei's parables are included in *The Wisdom of China and India.*

My favorite translation of the *Tao Teh Ching* is *Tao Teh King by Lao Tzu: Interpreted as Nature and Intelligence* by Archie Bahm (New York: Frederick Ungar Publishing Co., 1958).

My version of "A Farmer's Horse Ran Off" is based on a literary work titled "The Old Man at the Fort" by the Chinese prince and Taoist Liu An (178-122 B.C.E.) from his book *Huai Nan Tzu.* The tale gave rise to a popular Chinese saying:

> *sai weng shih ma*
> *yen chih fai fu*

(The old man lost his horse.
How could one know that it is not good fortune?)

The closest idiomatic expression to this saying in English is "a blessing in disguise."

The popular Chinese saying *sai weng shih ma* evokes the turn of events in the old tale. For comfort, when someone is having great sorrow, a friend might say only, "*Sai weng shih ma* (The old man lost his horse)." For balance, when someone is extremely elated about the turn of events, a friend might also say, "*Sai weng shih ma* (The old man lost his horse)." The rest would be understood. Versions of this story can be found in:

Chinese Fairy Tales and Fantasies by Moss Roberts (New York: Pantheon Books, 1979).
The Importance of Understanding: Translations from the Chinese by Lin Yutang (Cleveland: World Publishing Co., 1960).
The Eye of the Beholder, a sound recording by Heather Forest (Boston: Yellow Moon Press, 1990).

Special thanks to Danny Mao and David Chu for their helpful insights and translation.

ZEN STORIES FROM JAPAN

A MONK WITH HEAVY THOUGHTS

THE WILD STRAWBERRY

EMPTY-CUP MIND

A DISPUTE IN SIGN LANGUAGE

GIVING THE MOON

Although Siddhartha Gautama, the Buddha, was born in India around 563 B.C.E., the impact of his spiritual experience reverberated across the Far East during more than a thousand-year span. Traveling monks brought Buddhist teachings into China around 300 B.C.E. There these teachings blended with the mystical traditions of Taoism and transformed into Ch'an (meditation) Buddhism. By the year 500 C.E., as monks continued to travel eastward, Buddhist teachings reached Japan. By the twelfth century C.E., Ch'an Buddhism arrived, mingled with the poetic aesthetics of the Japanese culture, and became known as Zen. A spiritual tradition rich in koans, or stories, Zen Buddhist philosophy offers a profound collection of tales used in contemplative training.

"A Monk with Heavy Thoughts" is a story about non-attachment featuring Tanzan, a Zen master, and his distracted disciple, Ekido, who clings to his thoughts and cannot leave the past behind. Versions can be found as "Muddy Road" in *Zen Flesh Zen Bones* by Paul Reps (New York: Doubleday, 1989) and as "Crossing a Stream" in *Zen Koans* by Gyomay M. Kubose (Chicago: Henry Regnery Co., 1973).

"The Wild Strawberry" is a parable attributed to the Buddha. A version appears in *Zen Flesh Zen Bones* by Reps. Another printed version appears in a book titled *One Hand Clapping: Zen Stories for All Ages* by Rafe Martin (New York: Rizzoli, 1995).

"Empty-Cup Mind" is an anecdote told about Nan-in, a Zen master of the Meiji era (1868-1912) who served an overflowing cup of tea to an over-opinionated visiting professor. The story appears as "A Cup of Tea" in *Zen Flesh Zen Bones* by Reps and in *Zen Koans* by Kubose.

"A Dispute in Sign Language" is based on another story from Paul Reps's collection titled "Trading Dialogue for Lodging." A Jewish version on the theme of this story features a debate between a chicken seller and a despotic king. It can be found as "A Debate in Sign Language" in *Folktales of Israel* by Dov Noy (Chicago: University of Chicago Press, 1963). In both tales, a farcical comedy occurs when characters do not simply see what is in front of them.

"Giving the Moon" is a tale about the compassion of the Zen monk and poet Ryokan. Versions can be found as "The Moon Cannot Be Stolen" in *Zen Flesh Zen Bones* by Reps and in *Zen Koans* by Kubose.

TALES FROM ANCIENT GREECE

Aesop's Fables

ANTLERS

EVERYONE AGREES TO PEACE

MICE IN COUNCIL

Aesop was a storyteller who lived twenty-five hundred years ago in ancient Greece. Although Herodotus, the ancient Greek historian, mentions Aesop briefly in his writings, little is known for certain about him. Scholars differ about his origins. It has been said that Aesop was originally brought to Greece from Ethiopia as a slave. Because of his humble position in society, Aesop could not speak his thoughts openly. So he told fables, stories where animals speak and act like people. Through the voices of animal characters, Aesop safely said whatever he wished about human nature and the society around him. Legend has it that through his storytelling, Aesop gained freedom and rose to great renown and respect in his time.

Fables attributed to Aesop were preserved and passed down orally for centuries. Many ancient fables from India became intertwined with what we now call Aesop's fables when the Roman writer Valerius Babrius wrote prose versions in 230 C.E.

Versions of Aesop's fables can be found in:

Aesop's Fables: A New Version by Munro Leaf (New York: The Heritage Press, 1941).
Treasury of Aesop's Fables by Oliver Goldsmith (New York: Avenel Books, 1973).
New Tales from Aesop by Paul Roche (London: Honeyglen Publishing Limited, 1982).
The Fables of Aesop by Joseph Jacobs (London: Macmillan & Co., 1910).

Tales of Mount Olympus

BAUCIS AND PHILEMON

ECHO AND NARCISSUS

The Roman poet Ovid is the written source of the Greek tale of "Baucis and Philemon," which celebrates the everlasting qualities of true love and applauds giving one's best effort. In Ovid's version, the Roman names Jupiter and Mercury are used for the Greek gods Zeus and Hermes. Other printed versions of the tale can be found in *Mythology: Timeless Tales of Gods and Heroes* by Edith Hamilton (New York: The New American Library, 1940) and in *Bulfinch's Mythology: The Age of Fable, the Age of Reason and the Legends of Charlemagne* by Thomas Bulfinch (New York: Thomas Y. Crowell Co., 1970).

Other versions of "Echo and Narcissus," a Greek cautionary tale about the danger of self-infatuation and idle chatter, can be found in *The Book of Greek Myths* by Edgar Parin and Ingri D'Aulaire (Garden City, N.Y.: Doubleday and Co., 1962) and in *Bulfinch's Mythology: The Age of Fable, the Age of Reason and the Legends of Charlemagne* by Bulfinch.

TALES FROM THE MIDDLE EAST
Sufi Stories of Mulla Nasrudin

THE BOATMAN

THE SMUGGLER

FEEDING HIS CLOTHES

LOOKING FOR THE KEY

Mulla Nasrudin is both a wise and foolish character who appears in thousands of anecdotal tales told by storytellers throughout the Middle East. Incorporated into the mystical Sufi tradition, Mulla Nasrudin's comical antics shed light on the everyday foibles of human beings. In Persian, the word *mulla* means "a learned man" or "a teacher." Mulla is sometimes portrayed as a wise man offering sage advice to his followers, while in other tales he is a bumbling fool, whose charm lies in the thought-provoking, zany solutions he finds for his problems.

Although he is a legendary figure and is referred to by other names such as Nasrettin Hoca in Turkey and Khaji Nasriddin in other parts of the Middle East, tales of his comical exploits are likely a composite made by humorists through the ages. Many Middle Eastern cultures have claimed him for their own. In Turkey, some say he was born in 1208 in the village of Khurto, while others insist his birthplace was Eskisehir, where there is an annual Nasrudin Festival.

Generally, tales featuring Mulla are humorous and yet contain a poignant philosophic point. By opening the listener's heart with laughter, the tales create a space for a wise thought to enter. Indries Shah, a noted scholar on the mystical Sufi sect, states, "The Sufis, who believe that deep intuition is the only real guide to knowledge, use these stories almost like exercises. They ask people to choose a few which especially appeal to them, and to turn them over in the mind, making them their own. Teaching masters of the dervishes say that in this way a breakthrough into a higher wisdom can be effected." (*The Exploits of the Incomparable Mulla Nasrudin* [London: Pan Books, 1973].)

Most people, however, who have retold Mulla stories in bazaars and around dinner tables throughout the Middle East have used them for the pleasure of an enjoyable tale. By tradition, if you tell one Mulla tale, another must be told until several are recounted. Printed versions of Sufi stories can be found in:

Classic Tales of Mulla Nasreddin by Houman Farzad, translated by Diane L. Wilcox (Costa Mesa, Calif.: Mazda Publishers, 1989).

The Pleasantries of the Incredible Mulla Nasrudin by Indries Shah (New York: E.G. Dutton & Co., 1971).

The Exploits of the Incomparable Mulla Nasrudin by Indries Shah (London: Pan Books, 1973).

TALES FROM THE JEWISH TRADITION

FEATHERS (EASTERN EUROPE—HASIDIC)

THIS TOO SHALL PASS (ANCIENT ISRAEL—A KING SOLOMON LEGEND)

THE WOODEN SWORD (AFGHANISTAN)

Jewish literature begins with the Torah (the Five Books of Moses), which contains basic Jewish law. Numerous texts and commentary have been added to the body of Jewish written law over the centuries. Teacher-scribes, called Tannaim, wrote the Mishna, or oral doctrines, over a five-hundred-year period. Futher commentary, or explanation, of these texts was added as the Talmud, which is rich with illustrative stories. The Talmud is a collection of many books written by Jewish religious scholars and examines the text of the Mishna line by line.

There are two Talmuds, one completed in Babylonia in the fifth century C.E. and another shorter one completed earlier in Jerusalem. Each Talmud has two elements, the Halacha, or the law, and the Agada, an interpretation of scripture through storytelling. Simultaneously to the creation of the Mishna, another body of written work was created by the Tannaim scribes. Since religious law forbade the early Jews of Babylonia from using the plastic arts to celebrate Deity, the art of storytelling in the form of parables, or Midrash, flourished. The Midrash was compiled by scribes over time, until the great Jewish schools of Babylonia were closed in 1040 C.E. With the invention of the printing press about 1450 by Gutenberg, tales from both the Agada and the Midrash became more widely accessible as Jewish folklore was printed in Yiddish. The Hasidic movement of the eighteenth century added colorful parables and wonder tales to the Hebrew oral tradition.

FEATHERS (EASTERN EUROPE—HASIDIC)

The tale of "Feathers" is an Eastern European Jewish folktale that has been told over the centuries by both teachers and modern storytellers to celebrate the power of the spoken word. It is a cautionary tale that, through simple yet graphic imagery, points out how carefully we must consider our words. Once freed from the lips, words cannot be swallowed up again. This Hasidic tale, attributed to Rabbi Levi Yitzhak of Berditchev, can also be found in *Who Knows Ten* by Molly Cone (New York: Union of American Hebrew Congregations, 1965). My version also appears in *Chosen Tales* by Peninnah Schram (Northvale, N.J.: Jason Aronson, 1995).

THIS TOO SHALL PASS (ANCIENT ISRAEL—A KING SOLOMON LEGEND)

This King Solomon legend is widely told. Although ancient, this tale resonates in modern times. The sale of good luck rings with the letters *gzy* inscribed on them raised money for a company of soldiers who served in World War II. The letters were a reference to this story, which gives the Hebrew phrase *Gam Zeh Ya'avor,* "This too shall pass." Other printed versions of the tale can be found in *Tales from the Wise Men of Israel* by Judith Ish-Kishor (New York: J.P. Lippincott Company, 1962) and in *Folktales of Israel* by Dov Noy (Chicago: University of Chicago Press, 1963).

THE WOODEN SWORD (AFGHANISTAN)

Since ancient times, Jewish culture has been filled with stories. The Diaspora took Jewish folklore throughout the world. The tale of "The Wooden Sword" was collected in Afghanistan and features Shah Abbas, disguised as a dervish, who encounters a poor Jew in his community. A popular tale told by contemporary storytellers, the plot turns on the basic premise of optimism. Each time disaster threatens the happiness of the Hebrew character in this tale, the poor man reminds himself, "Day by day, all will be well." His refreshing outlook helps him to reach a high position as an adviser to the ruler of the land. Versions of this tale can be found in *The Classic Tales: 4000 Years of Jewish Lore* by Ellen Frankel (Northvale, N.J.: Jason Aronson, 1993) and in *Gates to the Old City* by Raphael Patai (Northvale, N.J.: Jason Aronson, 1988).

TALES FROM THE CHRISTIAN TRADITION

THE LEGEND OF ST. GENESIUS

AMAZING GRACE: THE STORY OF JOHN NEWTON (1725-1807)

THE PRODIGAL SON: A PARABLE FROM THE NEW TESTAMENT

THE LEGEND OF ST. GENESIUS

I first heard the story behind the expression "break a leg" from Ed Stivender, storyteller, theological scholar, and author of *Raised Catholic (Can You Tell?)* (Little Rock, Ark.: August House, 1992). He shared the story after giving me an oval St. Genesius medal. I still store this small engraving with my most treasured jewels. A print version of this saint tale can be found in *Saints Preserve Us!: Everything You Need to Know about Every Saint You'll Ever Need* by Sean Kelly and Rosemary Rogers (New York: Random House, 1993).

AMAZING GRACE: THE STORY OF JOHN NEWTON (1725-1807)

The Christian hymn "Amazing Grace," written over two hundred years ago, has long been a popular song in churches in the American South. During the folk music revival of the sixties, folk artists recorded the hymn, and it entered the mainstream of popular culture. Although it is often sung at commemorative events and religious gatherings, the history behind the song is not commonly known. Many new verses have been added over the years. The hymn and a version of its history can be found in *Amazing Grace: The Story*

Behind the Song by Jim Haskin (Brookfield, Conn.: The Millbrook Press, 1992) and in *Rise Up Singing* by Peter Blood-Patterson (Bethlehem, Pa.: Sing-Out Publications, 1989).

THE PRODIGAL SON: A PARABLE FROM THE NEW TESTAMENT

The story of the prodigal son appears in the New Testament in the Gospel of Luke, chapter 15, verses 11–32. It is a parable, or a metaphorical tale with many layers of meaning, told by Jesus of Nazareth to his disciples to offer insight into the Kingdom of Heaven. My redaction, or edited version of the story, is based on the translation from the Greek in *The Holy Bible: Revised Standard Version* (New York: Thomas Nelson and Sons, 1946).

During times of great persecution, early Christians shared parables such as that of the prodigal son with each other to comfort those who had strayed and encourage them to return to the fold. The parable of the lost sheep, Luke, chapter 15, verses 3–7, sheds light on the meaning of this tale as it describes how a shepherd delights in finding the one small lamb who has gone astray. I have juxtaposed this Bible story with the tale behind the hymn "Amazing Grace," since, like the prodigal son, John Newton is a more recent example of one who was truly *lost* but was *found* again. For further commentary on this parable see *The New Bible Commentary*, edited by G. J. Wenham, J. A. Motyer, D. A. Carson, and R. T. France (Leicester, England: Inter-Varsity Press, 1953) or *Peake's Commentary on the Bible*, edited by Matthew Black (London: Thomas Nelson and Sons, 1962). Another redaction can be found in *The World's Wisdom: Sacred Texts of the World's Religions* by Philip Novak (San Franscisco: HarperCollins Publishers, 1994).

I give special thanks to Ed Stivender for his insights and consultation on the presentation of the Christian tales in this section.

TALES FROM AFRICA

FIRE, WATER, TRUTH, AND FALSEHOOD (NORTHEAST AFRICA—ETHIOPIA)

THE RED AND BLUE COAT (CENTRAL AFRICA—CONGO)

TONGUE MEAT (EAST-CENTRAL AFRICA—SWAHILI)

WHY WISDOM IS EVERYWHERE (WEST AFRICA—ASHANTI)

FIRE, WATER, TRUTH, AND FALSEHOOD (NORTHEAST AFRICA—ETHIOPIA)

This allegorical tale, in which ideas and things are presented with human characteristics, is told in Ethiopia and other Northeast African nations. Another printed version can be found in *The Fire on the Mountain and Other Ethiopian Stories* by Harold Courlander and Wolf Leslau (New York: Holt, Rinehart and Winston, 1950).

THE RED AND BLUE COAT (CENTRAL AFRICA—CONGO)

This metaphorical tale from the Congo graphically depicts one reason why battles begin between neighbors who interpret reality from different viewpoints. It is a folktale with current-event overtones. Violent conflicts occur all over the planet between people who live in proximity but do not share the same philosophies.

My retelling of this story is based on a version in *African Folktales* by Roger D. Abrahams (New York: Pantheon Books, 1983). A version in print can also be found in *Notes on the Folklore of the Fjort* by Richard Edward Dennett (London: The Folklore Society, 1894), along with other tales from the region and other detailed anthropological information. I first heard a variant of this tale from storyteller Diane Ferlatte.

TONGUE MEAT (EAST-CENTRAL AFRICA—SWAHILI)

The eastern coast of the African continent has long been a crossroads of Islamic and African culture. The result is a mix of the Bantu language and Islamic culture. For this reason one of the central characters in this tale is a sultan. The Swahili storytellers also tell comical stories of Abu Nuwasi that are reminiscent of Sufi stories featuring Mulla Nasrudin. Here, as in other places throughout Africa, the power of the spoken word is valued. Verbal eloquence is celebrated in this tale in which a poor man's stories and songs create health and beauty in his mate. A version of this tale along with other stories of the Swahili culture can be found in *Myths and Legends of the Swahili* by Jan Knappert (Nairobi: Heinemann Educational Books, 1970).

WHY WISDOM IS EVERYWHERE (WEST AFRICA—ASHANTI)

This tale features a trickster-hero character named Anansi the Spider, who is central to a large body of oral tales told by the Ashanti people along the coast of West Africa. He is generally a schemer whose unscrupulous deeds are eventually thwarted or punished. The tales are not overtly moral stories but indirectly discourage shameful behavior. Anansi is a spider with human-like characteristics and behavior who can often be seen creeping away to hide in corners.

African captives brought Anansi tales to North America, where they became the Aunt Nancy stories told in the southern United States. In Haiti, Anansi transformed into two characters, Bouki, who is the schemer, and Ti Malice, who is foolish. Through his colorful antics, Anansi the Spider sheds light on human folly and offers insights into appropriate behavior. Other printed versions of this tale can be found in *The Hat-Shaking Dance and Other Tales from the Gold Coast* by Harold Courlander (New York: Harcourt Brace and World, 1957) and in *Tales as Tools: The Power of Storytelling in the Classroom* by Sheila Daley (Jonesborough, Tenn.: The National Storytelling Press, 1994).

TALES FROM ASIA AND SOUTHEAST ASIA

THE PARTS OF THE HOUSE ARGUE (PHILIPPINES)

THE TIGER'S WHISKER (KOREA)

LITTLE LIZARD'S SORROW (VIETNAM)

THE PARTS OF THE HOUSE ARGUE (PHILIPPINES)

Since ancient times, kinship ties have been the basis for social community in the rural villages of the Philippine Islands. It is important that the members of a family who share a house live in harmony. If they quarrel, it is believed, terrible misfortune can befall everyone. Long ago a special ceremony called a *Sangasang* was held when a house was first built or when a house needed to be cured of its bad spirits. At the *Sangasang*, this tale about the parts of the house quarreling would be told. A version of the tale titled "Those Who Quarreled," along with other folklore of the Philippines, can be found in *Once in the First Times: Folktales from the Philippines* by Elizabeth Hough Secrists (Philadelphia: Macrae Smith Company, 1949).

Another similiar story on the theme of parts that argue about their relative importance can be found in an Aesop's fable titled "The Belly and the Members." In this tale, parts of the body realize the benefit of working together for the good of all. A version of this fable can be found in *The Favorite Book of Fables* (London: Thomas Nelson and Sons, 1890). A West African version on the theme of disputing parts that find peace in cooperation can be found as "We Oppose President Stomach" in *Animals Mourn for Da Leopard and Other West African Tales* by Peter G. Dorliae (Indianapolis: The Bobbs-Merrill Co., 1970).

THE TIGER'S WHISKER (KOREA)

This poignant tale has variants in both Africa and Southeast Asia. The tale offers sage advice on how loving patience can win the heart of someone who is having emotional difficulty. Although the tale is old, it reminds us of the emotional hardships faced by some contemporary soldiers who, after their war-time experiences, have difficulty assimilating into civilian life. A Korean version of this old plot appears in *The Tiger's Whisker* by Harold Courlander (New York: Harcourt, Brace and World, 1968). African versions, featuring a stepmother who attempts to win the love of her stepson by obtaining a lion's whisker for a similar love potion, can be found in *The Lion's Whisker: Tales of High Africa* by Brent Ashabranner and Russell Davis (Boston: Little, Brown & Co., 1959) and in *African Village Folktales* by Edna Mason Kaula (New York: World Publishing Co., 1968).

LITTLE LIZARD'S SORROW (VIETNAM)

In parts of Southeast Asia lives a tiny, gray lizard with suction feet that quickly climbs up and down the walls searching for insects to eat. It makes a human-like sound, as if someone is clicking his tongue on the roof of his mouth, saying, "Tsk, tsk, tsk." It is a noise some people make with their tongues when they shake their heads and express dismay about something. The human-like sound of this lizard once startled me as I sat in a living room in Indonesia, where it is called a *chingchok*. This is the tale I learned about why he scurries about so, making that curious sound.

My retelling of his tale is based on a version by author and illustrator Mai Vo-Dinh in *The Toad Is the Emperor's Uncle: Animal Folktales from Vietnam* (Garden City, N.Y.: Doubleday, 1970). Explanatory tales abound around the world. These stories often make indirect points about human nature. On one hand, this folktale explains how the little lizard, which in Vietnam is called a *than lan*, got its sound. But it also presents a wise character, the beggar, who understands the transience of life and does not equate who he is with what he owns.

TALES FROM EUROPE

THE THREE WISHES (ENGLAND)

THE WOODEN BOWL (GERMANY)

THE HAPPY MAN'S SHIRT (ITALY)

THE DANCING LASS OF ANGLESEY (SCOTLAND)

THE THREE WISHES (ENGLAND)

This tale offers a lighthearted comment on greed and the folly it can produce. Variations appear in England and France. Long ago in England, the royalty allotted only the fallen wood to the peasants. Sometimes shepherds would walk the royal forest with their long, hooked staffs held high so that they could knock off branches and render them into the "public domain." Hence, the expression "by hook or by crook" came into use. The tree fairy character is likely a reference to Silvanus, the animistic spirit who, according to the pagan world view, inhabited all trees. Other versions of this tale can be found in *The Three Wishes* by Charles Perrault (Mahwah, N.J.: Troll Books, 1979) and in *Best Loved Folktales of the World* by Joanna Cole (New York: Doubleday, 1982).

THE WOODEN BOWL (GERMANY)

"The Wooden Bowl" is based on the story titled "The Old Man and His Grandson" from *The Complete Grimm's Fairy Tales* (New York: Pantheon Books, 1944). This widely told tale speaks to the need for compassionate understanding between generations. The tale offers a sage reason for filial love and the acceptance of responsibility when frail elderly people become dependent on others for basic care. What goes around comes around.

A Romanian version that features a half blanket instead of a wooden bowl can be found in *Romanian Folk Tales* by Jean Ure (New York: Watts, 1960). An Italian version can be found in *Old Italian Tales* by Domenico Vittorini (New York: McKay, 1958).

THE HAPPY MAN'S SHIRT (ITALY)

This story, originally told about Alexander the Great in the Greek literary work *Pseudo-Callisthenes*, became a popular oral narrative in medieval times. A Danish version of the folktale inspired Hans Christian Andersen's similar tale, "The Shoes of Happiness." The Italian version was collected from an Italian housewife named Orsola Minon in 1912. Her version appears in *Italian Folktales* by Italo Calvino (New York: Pantheon Books, 1981). A children's book version can be found in *Once Upon a Time* by Rose Dobbs (New York: Random House, 1958). A Jewish version can be found in *Jewish Folktales: Selected and Retold* by Pinhas Sadeh (New York: Doubleday, 1989).

THE DANCING LASS OF ANGLESEY (SCOTLAND)

My retelling of this tale in verse is inspired by ballad No. 220, "The Bonny Lass of Anglesey," from *The English and Scottish Popular Ballads*, collected by Francis James Child, edited by Helen Child Sargent and George Lyman Kittredge (Boston: Houghton Mifflin Co., 1932). Similar plots appear in ballads from Denmark and Norway. A contemporary version, "The Bonny Lass of Anglesey," is sung by Martin Carthy to the Irish-American fiddle tune "Bonaparte's Retreat." I give special thanks to folksinger and storyteller Dan Keding, who introduced me to this feminist and pacifist tale featuring both a strong female protagonist and a sane alternative to the bloody competition of war.

TALES FROM THE AMERICAS

HOW WAR WAS ENDED (NORTH AMERICAN ARCTIC—CENTRAL YUP'IK ESKIMO)

HOW THE QUETZAL GOT ITS RED BREAST (CENTRAL AMERICA—MAYA)

OLD DOG AND COYOTE (MEXICO—OTOMI)

PACA AND BEETLE (SOUTH AMERICA—BRAZIL)

GLUSCABI AND THE MAGIC GAME BAG (NORTH AMERICAN EASTERN WOODLANDS—
    ABENAKI)

HOW WAR WAS ENDED (NORTH AMERICAN ARCTIC—CENTRAL YUP'IK ESKIMO)

This tale was told to me by Chuna McIntyre, a storyteller, singer, and dancer from the village of Eek in west-central Alaska. Chuna McIntyre is one of the few Yup'ik people who still know the songs, dances, and stories of his people. He is a highly respected performing artist and scholar who is helping to preserve the Yup'ik cultural tradition. He learned his songs and dances from his grandmother, who was a young girl at the time of the first contact with outsiders in 1898.

Many cultures have come to the awareness that war must end. Few, like the peaceful Yup'ik, have acted upon that awareness. Chuna McIntyre shared Apanugpak's story with me after he heard me sing my version of the Scottish ballad "The Dancing Lass of Anglesey" at the Bay Area Storytelling Festival in California. The song I sang, like the tale he told, describes a time when, instead of bloodshed, a dancing contest decides the winner of a battle.

The image of the ghosts of slain warriors in McIntyre's tale resonates powerfully with me as I consider the current wars around the planet whose roots reach into the distant past. Like "ghosts," terrible memories of old feuds fuel current atrocities, goading the children of the enemies into becoming enemies too. And, as Apanugpak so wisely realized, the score can never be settled as the numbers of slain warriors increase on both sides of the argument.

HOW THE QUETZAL GOT ITS RED BREAST (CENTRAL AMERICA—MAYA)

The quetzal is an endangered bird with colorful plumage whose habitat, the rain forests of Guatemala, is diminishing. By passing down this legend about the sacred quetzal, the Maya storytellers powerfully preserved a kernel of history about the devastation of their culture at the hands of the Spanish soldiers who came to their lands in the sixteenth century in search of gold.

The Maya are an ancient people who are among the original inhabitants of the Western Hemisphere. Their ancestors, dwelling long ago in what is now Mexico and Guatemala, developed an elaborate calendar that was the most accurate known until the currently used Gregorian calendar was introduced in 1582. The earliest Maya artifacts found by archaeologists date back to 1500 B.C.E. For mysterious reasons, around 900 C.E. a mass migration took place to what is now the Yucatan Peninsula in Mexico, leaving behind enormous square-based pyramids in Guatemala.

The Maya documented their knowledge of agriculture, weather, medicine, and advanced astronomy in ornate, carved stone writing. Ancient Maya hieroglyphs have only recently been decoded as the phonetic script of a spoken language.

Ancient Maya were also skilled weavers with developed techniques for spinning and dyeing cloth. Agriculture formed the basis of their economy, with cacao beans and copper bells being a source of monetary exchange. Skilled artisans, the ancient Maya crafted beautiful jewelry using the abundant gold, silver, jade, shells, and colorful bird plumage, especially quetzal feathers, found long ago in this area. Although the lifestyle of ancient times is gone, stories and folkways have preserved some of the culture.

Currently, over a million Maya live in the southern Mexican state of Chiapas. Nearly five million Maya live throughout the Yucatan, Belize, Guatemala, Honduras, and El Salvador. As modern archaeologists marvel over the remarkable accomplishments of the ancient Maya, contemporary descendants struggle for economic equality and basic human rights.

My retelling of the quetzal legend is based on information about the environmental plight of the Guatemalan quetzal found in "Mystical Messenger" by Diane Jukofsky in the *Nature Conservancy Magazine* 43 (November–December 1993): 25–29. Further information on the topic can be obtained from the Tropical Conservation Newsbureau, Rainforest Alliance, 65 Bleeker St., New York City, N.Y. 10012.

OLD DOG AND COYOTE (MEXICO—OTOMI)

This story features the trickster character Coyote, a prankster both wise and foolish who also appears in many North American native tales. My retelling of this story is based on a version told to me by Chouteau Chapin in Cushing, Me. She learned this story in the Mexican desert, when as a young woman she worked with the American Friends Service Committee as a teacher of native children. Her eyes twinkled as she leaned on her cane and recalled how the native children she taught long ago delighted in the lively animal sounds she always included when telling this tale. She explained to me that she had discovered the story in a hand-printed volume of stories collected by Baptist missionaries, who presented the tale in both its original Otomi language and Spanish.

The Otomi language is one of thirteen native languages once commonly spoken in Mexico. Others include Nahuatl and the Maya language from the Yucatan. The use of these languages has diminished since ancient times. Successive governments instituted programs to teach Spanish to all native peoples. Early Spanish missionaries collected native myths and stories in order to learn indigenous languages. An understanding of local language enabled missionaries to spread their own religious beliefs more easily.

PACA AND BEETLE (SOUTH AMERICA—BRAZIL)

This tale from Brazil is reminiscent of the Aesop's fable "The Tortoise and the Hare" with a few additional twists. Although it centers on a race between a fast and slow creature, the tale also explains how a beautiful beetle, which still can be found along the Amazon River, came to have its colors.

Stories travel as people travel. Certainly the roots of this plot are ancient and were likely brought to South America by travelers from across the Atlantic. As often happens with transported tales, new insights and details have been added to a familiar storyline. The tale we expect does not unfold. The slow creature wins, of course, but is not slow at all! Not everyone's talents are immediately obvious to others. In this story modesty and skill coexist in a ridiculed character who chooses not to brag.

Other printed versions of this fable can be found in *South American Wonder Tales* by Frances Carpenter (Chicago: Follett Publishing Co., 1969) and in her source, Elsie Spicer Eell's *Fairy Tales of Brazil*, 1917.

GLUSCABI AND THE MAGIC GAME BAG (NORTH AMERICAN EASTERN WOODLANDS— ABENAKI)

This tale, told by Abenaki storytellers, is old, and yet it resonates with contemporary ecological concerns. The Abenaki live in Vermont, New Hampshire, and in southern Quebec. Their tribal name means "People of the Dawn," for their traditional homeland is at the edge of the North American continent where one can see the first rays of sunrise over the ocean. Their story tradition features a character named Gluscabi, who long, long ago made himself out of some of the leftover dust of creation. When he was young, Gluscabi lived in a lodge with wise Grandmother Woodchuck, who helped him learn to live in balance with the earth and all living creatures. Because Gluscabi was young, he sometimes did foolish things. Fortunately, wise Grandmother Woodchuck always gave him helpful advice.

In traditional Abenaki culture, stories are an essential part of parenting. Abenaki parents do not hit their children in order to discipline them. That would be considered barbaric and cruel. They consider that the best teacher of proper behavior is a good example. But if that fails, Abenaki parents would simply tell a story to a child who needed a lesson. They believe that a story is a far more powerful tool than physical force to help a child understand acceptable behavior. Unlike physical force, which is humiliating and creates anger and fear in a child, stories gently work their way into the inner space of a young person and teach long after the telling.

Abenaki storytellers and parents often tell tales about Grandmother Woodchuck and Gluscabi, who when he was young, like many other children, did regrettable things. By telling stories about how wise Grandmother Woodchuck teaches Gluscabi to behave, Abenaki parents can subtly guide their own children to consider the consequences of their actions and choose appropriate behavior.

I give many thanks to Abenaki storyteller and author Joseph Bruchac for sharing insights into the culture of the Abenaki with me and for bringing this story to light in his book *Keepers of the Earth* (Golden, Colo.: Fulcrum Publishing, 1991). My retelling of the tale weaves the ecological perspective gained from Joseph Bruchac's retelling with the basic plot of the version found in "Penobscot Tales and Religious Beliefs" by Frank Speck in the *Journal of American Folklore* 38 (January–March 1935):39.

PROVERBS FROM AROUND THE WORLD

Proverbs are thought-provoking sayings or ideas that are memorable and are circulated orally because they contain some generally accepted truth. A proverb can be a powerful parenting tool, which, when spoken at an opportune moment, can make an unforgettable point. Proverbs are often passed down from one generation to the next in household settings. I invite readers to recall their own family's household proverbs. A familiar saying heard over and over in their homes during their growing years may come to mind. Assortments of world proverbs can be found in:

The Prentice-Hall Encyclopedia of World Proverbs: A Treasury of Wit and Wisdom Through the Ages, compiled by Wolfgang Mieder (Englewood Cliffs, N.J.: Prentice-Hall, 1986).

A Bird in the Hand: A Child's Guide to Sayings by Nigel Snell (London: H. Hamilton, 1986).

The Macmillan Book of Proverbs, Maxims, and Familiar Phrases, edited by Burton Egbert Stevenson (New York: Macmillan Co., 1965).

Too Many Cooks and Other Proverbs by Maggie Kneen (New York: Green Tiger Press, 1992).

Words from the Wise; Centuries of Proverbs to Live By, compiled by Arthur Wortman (Kansas City, Mo.: Hallmark, 1973).

Speak to the Winds: Proverbs from Africa, compiled by Kofi Asare Opoku (New York: Lothrop, Lee and Shepard, 1975).

The Concise Oxford Dictionary of Proverbs, edited by John Simpson (New York: Oxford University Press, 1992).

Proverbs Are Never out of Season by Wolfgang Mieder (New York: Oxford University Press, 1993).

ABOUT THE BORDER DESIGNS

The border designs for *Wisdom Tales from Around the World* and its companion volume, *Wonder Tales from Around the World,* were created by illustrator-designer David Boston of Hot Springs Village, Arkansas. They are based on traditional graphic motifs or textile patterns associated with the cultures or geographic regions from which the stories originate.

Special thanks to Liz Parkhurst, Jan Cottingham, Dinah Foglia, Robert Friedman, Rita Auerbach, Joseph Bruchac, Peninnah Schram, Ed Stivender, Chuna McIntyre, Rafe Martin, and Rabbi Arthur Schwartz for their insights, information, and generosity as this book evolved.

Multicultural Books and Audiobooks
from August House

Thirty-Three Multicultural Tales to Tell
Pleasant DeSpain
Hardback / ISBN 0-87483-265-9
Paperback / ISBN 0-87483-266-7
Audiobook / ISBN 0-87483-345-0

Twenty-Two Splendid Tales to Tell
Pleasant DeSpain
Paperback, volume I / ISBN 0-87483-340-X
Paperback, volume II / ISBN 0-87483-341-8

Wonder Tales From Around the World
Heather Forest
Hardback / ISBN 0-87483-421-X
Paperback / ISBN 0-87483-422-8
Audiobook / ISBN 0-87483-427-9

Of Kings and Fools
Stories of the French Tradition in North American
Michael Parent and Julien Olivier
Paperback / ISBN 0-87483-481-3

Cajun Folktales
J.J. Reneaux
Hardback / ISBN 0-87483-283-7
Paperback / ISBN 0-87483-282-9

Eleven Nature Tales
Pleasant DeSpain
Hardback / ISBN 0-87483-447-3
Paperback / ISBN 0-87483-458-9

August House Publishers, Inc.
P.O.Box 3223
Little Rock, Arkansas 72203
1-800-284-8784
FAX 501-372-5579
order@augusthouse.com

Other Books and Audiobooks from August House

Telling Your Own Stories
Donald Davis
Paperback / ISBN 0-87483-235-7

Healers on the Mountain
Native American stories with the power to heal
Teresa Pijoan
Paperback / ISBN 0-935305-269-1

Joseph the Tailor and Other Jewish Tales
Wisdom and wit of traditional Jewish and Biblical stories
Syd Lieberman
Audiobook / ISBN 0-87483-426-0

See Rock City
A Story Journey through Appalachia
Donald Davis
Hardback / ISBN 0-87483-448-1
Paperback / ISBN 0-87483-456-2
Audiobook / ISBN 0-87483-452-X

Listening for the Crack of Dawn
A Master Storyteller Recalls the Appalachia of the 50's & 60's
Donald Davis
Paperback / ISBN 0-87483-130-X
Audiobook / ISBN 0-87483-147-4

Thirteen Miles from Suncrest
Donald Davis
Hardback / ISBN 0-87483-379-5
Paperback / ISBN 0-87483-455-4

Barking at a Fox-Fur Coat
Family stories to keep you laughing into the next generation
Donald Davis
Hardback / ISBN 0-87483-140-7
Paperback / ISBN 0-87483-087-7

The Southern Bells
Donald Davis
Audiobook / ISBN 0-87483-390-6

Half-Horse, Half Alligator
The Roots of American Humor
Bill Mooney
Audiobook / ISBN 0-87483-494-5

August House Publishers, Inc.
P.O. Box 3223
Little Rock, Arkansas 72203
1-800-284-8784
FAX 501-372-5579
order@augusthouse.com